T0344483

INFORMATION PROCESSING
BY BIOCHEMICAL SYSTEMS

INFORMATION PROCESSING BY BIOCHEMICAL SYSTEMS

Neural Network–Type Configurations

ORNA FILO
NOAH LOTAN

The Leonard & Diane Sherman Center for Research in Biomaterials
Department of Biomedical Engineering
Technion–Israel Institute of Technology
Haifa, Israel

WILEY

A JOHN WILEY & SONS, INC., PUBLICATION

Published by John Wiley & Sons, Inc., Hoboken, New Jersey.
Published simultaneously in Canada.

For general information on our other products and services or for technical support, please contact our
Customer Care Department within the United States at (800) 762-2974, outside the United States at
(317) 572-3993 or fax (317) 572-4002.

Wiley also publishes its books in a variety of electronic formats. Some content that appears in print,
however, may not be available in electronic formats. For more information about Wiley products, visit
our web site at www.wiley.com.

Library of Congress Cataloging-in-Publication Data:

Filo, Orna.
   Information processing by biochemical systems : neural network–type configurations / Orna
Filo, Noah Lotan.
        p.   ;   cm.
   Includes bibliographical references and index.
   ISBN 978-0-470-50094-1 (cloth)
   1. Biocomputers.   2. Neural networks (computer science)   3. Information technology.
I. Lotan, Noah.   II. Title.
   [DNLM: 1. Automatic Data Processing.   2. Biochemical Phenomena.   3. Neural Networks
(Computer) QU 26.5 F478i 2010]
   QA76.884.F55 2010
   006.3'2–dc22

                                                                        2009019358

Printed in the United States of America

10 9 8 7 6 5 4 3 2 1

In Memoriam

CONTENTS

PREFACE

Information processing by biological systems is not an invention of the modern era. It started in the far past with the semblance of life on our planet, was operative in single-celled organisms, and was active throughout the ages with the evolution of higher species.

During the last few decades this area of endeavor has attracted the attention of scientists and engineers. They were driven not only by the inborn curiosity of human beings, but also by the quest for solutions to practical issues. Among the latter, the most pressing were the miniaturization of devices and conferring upon them greatly extended capabilities for information processing. More recently, as sustained efforts were aimed at these goals, a critical warning was issued by physicists. They pointed out that, sooner or later, the technology currently available is bound to reach the limits of its capabilities. This will be caused by undesired crosstalk between the densely packed ultraminiaturized components, as well as by the inability to dissipate the heat produced. Hence, alternative technologies had to be developed. It was at this point that the concepts of information processing by molecular systems emerged—among them, biomolecular systems.

This book is not intended to present either a summary of the historical developments in the area of concern or a full and detailed account of more recent accomplishments. Rather, it is intended to present to the reader the progress achieved in a limited section of this area and, particularly, the relationship prevailing between two apparently unrelated fields. One field encompasses defined biochemical systems whose performance can be understood and described in the rigorous terms of biochemical engineering. The other is concerned with the concepts of neural networks, which are now fundamental in efforts made to understand the functioning of human brains. As such, this book is just one stop on a long journey.

It is also our intention that the book will stir the interest of scholars involved in related areas and in so doing we invite them to expand research in the field of concern. To this end, the language of the book is somewhat didactic. Moreover, a wealth of information is included regarding both the experimental aspects (i.e., materials and equipment used) and computational procedures involved.

The content of this book is taken in part from the Ph.D. Thesis of Orna Filo, submitted to the Technion–Israel Institute of Technology, in Haifa, Israel.

The research described was performed at the Leonard & Diane Sherman Center for Research in Biomaterials, in the Department of Biomedical Engineering.

ORNA FILO
NOAH LOTAN

TERMINOLOGY

Basic System

The basic system is an enzymic system including enzymes, substrates, cofactors, and products that functions according to well-defined rules. The basic system receives input, carries information-processing operations on this input, and produces an output.

Input

The input consists of (1) data (flow rates and concentrations of substrates, cofactors, and products), (2) mode of operation of the system, and (3) kinetic characteristics of the enzymic system.

Information

Information consists of (1) part of the input that is processed in the basic system or in the biochemical network (i.e., concentration profiles of substrates and cofactors) and (2) part of the output produced by the basic system or the biochemical network (i.e., concentration profiles of products, substrates, and cofactors). The information is a signal defined by its type, frequency, and amplitude.

Output

The output consists of flow rates and concentrations of substrates, cofactors, and products.

Information Processing

The system performs information processing when the information obtained in the output is different from the information fed in the input in at least one of its characteristics (i.e., signal type, frequency, or amplitude).

Biochemical Network

In a biochemical network, several basic systems are connected to one another. The connection is achieved by the fact that the information contained in the output of one basic system is fed as input into another basic system. For example, the product of one basic system is also the substrate of the basic system connected to it.

LIST OF SYMBOLS AND ACRONYMS

Symbols

A	Cofactor consumed in reaction (1)
A_i	Cofactor taking part in the ith basic system of a biochemical network
[A]	Concentration of A in a fed-batch reactor
$[A]_i$	Concentration of A in compartment i of a continuous reactor
$[A_i]$	Concentration of cofactor A_i
B	Cofactor consumed in reaction (2)
B_i	Cofactor taking part in the ith basic system of a biochemical network
[B]	Concentration of B in a fed-batch reactor
$[B]_i$	Concentration of B in compartment i of a continuous reactor
$[B_i]$	Concentration of cofactor B_i
C_j	Concentration of component j in a fed-batch reactor
$C_{j,0}$	Concentration of component j in the feed stream
$C_{j,i}$	Concentration of component j in compartment i of a continuous reactor
E_1	Enzyme catalyzing reaction (1)
$[E_1]$	Concentration of E_1 in a fed-batch reactor
$[E_1]_i$	Concentration of E_1 in compartment i of a continuous reactor
E_2	Enzyme catalyzing reaction (2)
$[E_2]$	Concentration of E_2 in a fed-batch reactor
$[E_2]_i$	Concentration of E_2 in compartment i of a continuous reactor

E_i	Enzyme catalyzing reaction i in a biochemical network
$[E_i]$	Concentration of E_i
I	External inhibitor
$[I]_0$	Concentration of I in the feed stream
$[I]_i$	Concentration of I in compartment i of a continuous reactor
K_a	Equilibrium dissociation constant for reaction (1)
K_b	Equilibrium dissociation constant for reaction (2)
K_{eq}	Equilibrium constant
K_{m,S_1}	Michaelis constant for S_1
K_{m,S_2}	Michaelis constant for S_2
$K_{m,A}$	Michaelis constant for A
$K_{m,B}$	Michaelis constant for B
K_{m,P_1}	Michaelis constant for P_1
K_{m,P_2}	Michaelis constant for P_2
$K_{m,j}$	Michaelis constant for component j
$K_{b,1}$	Inhibition constant for reaction (1)
$K_{q,1}$	Inhibition constant for reaction (1)
$K_{b,2}$	Inhibition constant for reaction (2)
$K_{q,2}$	Inhibition constant for reaction (2)
K_{i,S_1}	Inhibition constant for S_1
$K_{i,A}$	Inhibition constant for A
$K_{i,B}$	Inhibition constant for B
K_I	Inhibition constant for the external inhibitor
$K_{i,G6P}$	Inhibition constant for the inhibitor G6P
$K_{i,NADPH}$	Inhibition constant for the inhibitor NADPH
L_1	The minimum value of the concentrations of S_1 and S_2 in the feed stream ($[S_1]_0$ and $[S_2]_0$)
L_2	The maximum value of the concentrations of S_1 and S_2 in the feed stream ($[S_1]_0$ and $[S_2]_0$)
P_1	Product produced in reaction (1)
$[P_1]$	Concentration of P_1 in a fed-batch reactor
$[P_1]_i$	Concentration of P_1 in compartment i of a continuous reactor
P_2	Product produced in reaction (2)
$[P_2]$	Concentration of P_2 in a fed-batch reactor
$[P_2]_i$	Concentration of P_2 in compartment i of a continuous reactor
P_i	Product produced in reaction i in a biochemical network
$[P_i]$	Concentration of P_i
Q_j	Volumetric flow rate of the inlet stream feeding component j
Q	Volumetric flow rate
r_j	Rate of production of component j by reaction
$r_{j,i}$	Rate of production of component j by reaction in the ith compartment of a continuous reactor

r_1	Rate of reaction (1) in a fed-batch reactor
$r_{1,i}$	Rate of reaction (1) in the ith compartment of a continuous reactor
r_2	Rate of reaction (2) in a fed-batch reactor
$r_{2,i}$	Rate of reaction (2) in the ith compartment of a continuous reactor
r_i	Rate of reaction i in a biochemical network
S_1	Substrate consumed in reaction (1)
$[S_1]$	Concentration of S_1 in a fed-batch reactor
$[S_1]_0$	Concentration of S_1 in the feed stream
$[S_1]_i$	Concentration of S_1 in compartment i of a continuous reactor
S_2	Substrate consumed in reaction (2)
$[S_2]$	Concentration of S_2 in a fed-batch reactor
$[S_2]_0$	Concentration of S_2 in the feed stream
$[S_2]_i$	Concentration of S_2 in compartment i of a continuous reactor
S_i	Substrate consumed in reaction i in a biochemical network
$[S_i]$	Concentration of S_i
$[S_i]_0$	Concentration of S_i in the feed stream
t	Time
V	Volume of the reaction mixture
V_0	Initial volume of the reaction mixture
V_i	Volume of the ith compartment in a continuous reactor
$V_{m,1}$	Maximum rate of reaction (1)
$V_{m,2}$	Maximum rate of reaction (2)
$V_{m,-1}$	Maximum rate of reaction (1r) in the reverse direction
$V_{m,-2}$	Maximum rate of reaction (2r) in the reverse direction
$V_{m,i}$	Maximum rate of reaction i
$V_{m,G6PDH}$	Maximum rate of the reaction catalyzed by G6PDH
$V_{m,GR}$	Maximum rate of the reaction catalyzed by GR

Greek Symbols

π	Cycle time
τ	Period time

Acronyms

ADH	Alcohol dehydrogenase
ANN	Artificial neural networks
CSTR	Continuous stirred tank reactor
G6P	D-Glucose-6-phosphate
G6PDH	Glucose-6-phosphate dehydrogenase
GDH	Glucose dehydrogenase

GR	Glutathione reductase
GSH	Glutathione, reduced form
GSSG	Glutathione, oxidized form
LDH	L-Lactate dehydrogenase
NAD	Nicotinamide adenine dinucleotide
NADH	Nicotinamide adenine dinucleotide, reduced form
NADP	Nicotinamide adenine dinucleotide phosphate
NADPH	Nicotinamide adenine dinucleotide phosphate, reduced form
PFR	Plug flow reactor

1

INTRODUCTION AND LITERATURE SURVEY

1.1 INTRODUCTION

Both living organisms and computers are "information-processing machines" that operate on the basis of internally stored programs, but the differences between these systems are also quite large. In the case of living organisms, self-assembly occurs following an internal program, and the nervous system and brain formed in this way function as an autonomous information machine. Unlike traditional computers which must be "driven" from the outside, biological systems have somehow incorporated within them rules on how to function. Moreover, in the case of biological entities for which there is no external blueprint, the design plan is entirely internal and is thought to undergo changes both in the evolution of species and in the development of individuals. These similarities and differences have drawn the attention of computer scientists as well as of life scientists.

In order to revolutionize the current world of computers, three roads, or any combinations of them, are clearly visible [1]

1. Changing the physical elements at the foundations of the computer components
2. Changing the architecture of computers
3. Devising new software and computing algorithms

Information Processing by Biochemical Systems: Neural Network–Type Configurations, By Orna Filo and Noah Lotan
Copyright © 2010 John Wiley & Sons, Inc.

It is, however, true that a biological computer (or *biocomputer*) of a completely different nature from today's electronic computers already exists in the form of the fundamental phenomenon of life. The most advanced machinery, a living organism, operates with functional elements that are of molecular dimensions and actually exploits the quantum-size effects of its components [1]. Yet the quintessentially biological functions of living forms: autonomy, self-organization, self-replication, and development, as witnessed in both evolution and individual ontogeny, are completely absent from current computing machines [1].

Two major approaches to the construction of a biocomputer are reviewed here:

1. Study of the operational mechanism of biological systems, particularly those of the living brain, and the use of these results in the redesign of computer software and hardware architecture based on semiconductor technology (Section 1.2).
2. Development of biocomponents that are similar to and/or composed of biological macromolecules, the development of biochips that make use of these components, and ultimately, the construction of biocomputers (Section 1.3).

1.2   COMPUTATIONAL PROCESSES BASED ON BIOLOGICAL PRINCIPLES

1.2.1   Modeling Biological Processes

The involvement of biology might lead to new computational processes based on those found in natural systems. Multiple modes of processing contribute to the information-processing functions of biological systems, and these have been investigated and modeled extensively [2–8]. In his pioneering work, Rosen [9,10] introduced a two-factor model based on the idea that the fundamental dynamic behavior of physiological and biochemical systems is regulated by the combined action of two factors, one excitatory and the other inhibitory. Kampfner, Kirby, and Conrad [11–13] introduced theoretical models of enzymic neuron systems for learning processes, based on the concept of a hypothetic enzyme called excitase. Based on the same concept, a comprehensive mathematical model of the enzymic neuron as a logical circuit has been introduced by Neuschl and Menhart [14].

1.2.2   Artificial Neural Networks

The nerve cell has proved to be an extremely valuable source of ideas about networks of automata. A fundamentally different approach to computation is represented by artificial neural networks (ANNs), which are designed to mimic the basic organizational features of biological nervous systems [15–22]. The building brick of any neural computing system is some sort of representation of the fundamental cell of the brain: the neuron. Thus, ANNs consist of a large number of simple interconnected processing elements which are simplified models of neurons, and the interconnections between the processing elements are simplified models of the synapses between neurons. The processing of information in such networks occurs in parallel and is distributed throughout each unit composing the network [15–22].

There has been a steady development of neuronal analogs over the past 50 years. An important early model was proposed in 1943 by McCulloch and Pitts [23]. They described the neuron as a logical processing unit, and the influence of their model set the mathematical tone of what is being done today. Adaption or learning is a major focus of neural net research. The development of a learning rule that could be used for neural models was pioneered by Hebb, who proposed the famous Hebbian model for synaptic modification [24]. Since then, many alternative quantitative interpretations of synaptic modification have been developed [15–22].

There is no universally accepted definition of an artificial neural network. However, some definitions can be found in the literature, and examples are cited here.

- Robert Hecht-Nielsen, the inventor of one of the first commercial neurocomputers, defined [17] a *neural network* as "a computing system made up of a number of simple, highly interconnected processing elements, which process information by its dynamic state response to external inputs."
- According to the *DARPA Neural Network Study* [18]: "A neural network is a system composed of many simple processing elements operating in parallel whose function is determined by network structure, connection strengths, and the processing performed at computing elements or nodes."
- According to Aleksander and Morton [19], *neural computing* can be defined as "the study of networks of adaptable nodes which, through a process of learning from task examples, store experiential knowledge and make it available for use."
- According to Zurada [20], artificial neural systems, or neural networks, are "physical cellular systems which can acquire, store, and utilize experiential knowledge."
- According to Nigrin [21], "a neural network is a circuit composed of a very large number of simple processing elements that are neurally based. Each element operates only on local information. Furthermore

each element operates asynchronously; thus, there is no overall system clock."
- Haykin [22] offers a definition based on Aleksander and Morton [19]: "A neural network is a massively parallel distributed processor that has a natural propensity for storing experiential knowledge and making it available for use. It resembles the brain in two respects:
  - Knowledge is acquired by the network through a learning process.
  - Interneuron connection strengths known as synaptic weights are used to store the knowledge."

Significant progress in neural network research has been made in recent decades [15–22,25]. Presently, the neural network strategy is implemented at either the software or hardware level. The VLSI (very large scale integration) version of neural network implementation is a technology that has approached a certain degree of maturity [22]. Although the VLSI version serves as an impressive demonstration of the power of the new computer architecture of neural networks, it falls short of a radical design departure that is capable of capturing the structural and functional flexibility inherent in biosystems [25]. Many experts believe that neural network technology will be more robust and more powerful when its implementation becomes possible in a molecular-based "hardware" environment [25].

1.3   MOLECULAR AND BIOMOLECULAR ELECTRONICS

1.3.1   Motivation

The high-technology revolution that made the personal computer standard equipment was fueled primarily by astonishing advances in microelectronics that allow more and more circuit elements to be packed into a small integrated circuit (IC). The number of device components packaged into a single IC has grown exponentially with the passage of time [25–28]. Moreover, we witness increasing capability of each IC, increasing speed of operation, reduced consumption of energy, reduction in sizes and weights of the finished products, and reduced prices. Will this trend continue so that the device size eventually reaches the atomic scale? To many experts the answer is "not if using conventional microelectronics technology," which exploits mainly macroscopic properties of inorganic materials, because the ensuing quantum size and the thermal effects will make such devices unreliable [25,28]. Thus, today, the miniaturization and integration of electronic devices are being pushed to their physical limits [25–28].

1.3.2   Molecular Electronics

Molecular electronics is defined broadly as the encoding, manipulation, and retrieval of information at a molecular or macromolecular level [25–29]. This approach contrasts with current techniques, in which these functions are accomplished via lithographic manipulations of bulk materials to generate integrated circuits [28]. A key advantage of the molecular approach is the ability to design and fabricate devices from the bottom-up, on an atom-by-atom basis. Lithography can never provide the level of control available through organic synthesis or genetic engineering [28]. The molecular primitives allow for improvement in a number of information-processing device characteristics compared with similar characteristics of silicon-based devices. Thus, molecular information processing is attractive because it offers [29]:

- Integrability at the atomic scale
- High computational speed due to parallel processing, which compensates for the inherent low processing rate of each elementary device
- Self-assembly capability of atomic or molecular processors
- Plasticity of the molecular circuit, which can reconfigure itself to optimize its performance, taking into account the previous experience (learning)
- Fault-tolerance capability and even self-repair ability of the molecular circuit
- Reduced power consumption

Since Aviram's proposal of a molecular rectifier [30,31], a variety of designs of molecular electronic devices have appeared. Molecular-scale devices are fabricated on the nanometer scale and are composed of either a single molecule or several molecules configured into a supramolecular complex. Among these devices, molecular rectifiers, molecular switches, molecular diodes, molecular photodiodes, and molecular memories are described [30–39]. Studies also deal with assembling the individual components in thin-film configurations [25,40,41], forming artificial membranes [25,42] and establishing an interface between the molecules and conventional electronic materials [43]. Another possibility that has been investigated is the use of electroconductive polymers as "molecular wires" for establishing the connection required between molecular elements [43,44].

1.3.3   Biomolecular Electronics

Biomolecular electronics is a subfield of molecular electronics that considers the use of native and modified biological molecules in electronic or photonic devices [45–56]. The growing interest in the possibility of utilizing biological molecules in molecular electronics is fostered by the basic understanding that, in so doing, one may be able to take advantage of the specific characteristics and unique capabilities of these natural molecules [44–56]. Among the biomolecular devices investigated, protein-based molecular devices have gained increasing attention due to the versatile and highly specific molecular functionality of proteins [43,57]. Enzymes [44,58–67], receptors [68], antibodies [43], and bacteriorhodopsin [29,69–73] have been used as either electronic or optical devices. Computation with simple DNA manipulations has also been demonstrated [74,75].

1.4   BIOCHEMICAL DEVICES BASED ON ENZYMIC REACTIONS

In an extensive study, Okamoto and co-workers [76–86] introduced a biochemical switching device based on a cyclic enzyme system in which two enzymes share two cofactors in a cyclic manner. Cyclic enzyme systems have been used as biochemical amplifiers to improve the sensitivity of enzymatic analysis [87–89], and subsequently, this technique was introduced into biosensors [90–93]. In addition, cyclic enzyme systems were also widely employed in enzymic reactors, in cases where cofactor regeneration is required [94–107]. Using computer simulations, Okamoto and associates [77,80–83] investigated the characteristics of the cyclic enzyme system as a switching device, and their main model characteristics and simulation results are detailed in Table 1.1, as is a similar cyclic enzyme system introduced by Hjelmfelt et al. [109,116], which can be used as a logic element.

Subsequently, Okamoto and associates [84–86] investigated the connection of several cyclic enzyme systems in order to construct a network. In their models the cyclic enzyme system represents a biochemical neuron that participates in a biochemical neural network. These models are detailed in Table 1.2. Theoretical models of such networks were also proposed by Hjelmfelt and co-workers [109–111,116], and these are also presented in Table 1.2.

Models for biochemical switches, logic gates, and information-processing devices that are also based on enzymic reactions but do not use the cyclic enzyme system were also introduced [76,115,117–122]. Examples of these models are presented in Table 1.3. It should also be mentioned that in other studies [108,112–114,116], models of chemical neurons and chemical neural networks based on nonenzymic chemical reactions were also introduced.

Table 1.1 Models Based on the Cyclic Enzyme System

Model No.	Model Characteristics	Results	Conclusions and Applications	Comments[a]	Refs.
1	(Diagram: cyclic enzyme system with $I_1 \to X_1$, k_1, X_2, k_3, I_2, X_3, k_2, X_4, k_4, and cycle $A \to B$) I_1, I_2: inputs to the system's substrate pools of X_1 and X_3, respectively. Simple mass action kinetics. Irreversible reactions.	The steady-state concentrations of A and B ($\overline{A}$, $\overline{B}$) change stepwise at $I_2/I_1 = 1$ and can be represented as $\overline{A} = f(I_1, I_2)$ $= [1 \text{ if } I_1 \geq I_2;\ 0 \text{ if } I_1 < I_2]$ The steady-state concentrations of X_2 and X_4 ($\overline{X}_2$, $\overline{X}_4$) are also a function of I_1 and I_2: $\overline{X}_2 = \overline{X}_4 = f(\min(I_2, I_2))$ $= \left[\frac{1}{k} \text{ if } I_1 \geq I_2;\ \frac{1}{k} \text{ if } I_1 < I_2\right]$ where k indicates the rate constant of the decay of X_2 or X_4, k_3 or k_4, respectively.		The mathematical equations for this model and the following ones agree with the case of batch reactions, in which there is no mass flow into or out of the system. However, I_1 and I_2 cannot be defined as mass flows if volume changes are not considered.	77
2	(Diagram: cyclic enzyme system with $I_1 \to X_1$, E_1, X_2, k_3, I_2, X_3, E_2, X_4, k_4, and cycle $A \to B$) Same assumptions as in model 1 except: Reaction mechanisms are assumed to be ordered bi–bi enzymic reactions.	Same results for X_2 and X_4 as obtained in model 1.			77

(continued)

Table 1.1 (continued)

Model No.	Model Characteristics	Results	Conclusions and Applications	Comments[a]	Refs.
3	Same assumptions as in model 1 except: I_1 and I_2 change linearly with time such that $I_1(t) = 80 + t$ $I_2(t) = 100 - t$	X_2 and X_4 are dynamically regulated by the levels of I_1 and I_2 as described in model 1. Switching of dependence on the inputs at a point beyond the similar point determined by the steady-state analysis is observed. This time lag is due to an accumulation of X_3. Concentrations of A(t) and B(t) show a step function with the same time lag as X_2 and X_4.	The dynamic behavior of the cyclic enzyme system display catastrophic behavior in response to specific changes in external input. The system can realize a neuronic model capable of storing memory.		77,82
4	Same assumptions as in model 1 except: I_1 and I_2 are represented by a sinusoidal function with time t, such that $I_1(t) = 10 + 2\sin\left(\frac{2\pi}{40}t + \frac{\pi}{2}\right)$ $I_2(t) = 10 + 2\sin\left(\frac{2\pi}{40}t - \frac{\pi}{2}\right)$	Concentrations of A(t) and B(t) follow the pattern described in models 1 and 2. The time lag is observed due to accumulation of X_1 and X_3. Switching does not occur until the accumulation of either substrate is canceled.	The accumulated substrate is equivalent to a "condenser" and is applicable to a kind of "memory storage."		81
5	(reaction scheme): $I_1 \xrightarrow{} X_1 \xrightarrow{k_1} X_2 \xrightarrow{k_3}$, $X_1 \uparrow k_5$, $k_4 \downarrow X_4 \xleftarrow{k_2} X_3$, $X_3 \xrightarrow{k_6}$, $X_3 \xrightarrow{} I_2$, cycle $A \to B$; Same assumptions as in model 4 except: $k_5 \neq 0$ and $k_6 \neq 0$.	No time lag is observed, and the conversion from switched on to off (or from off to on) occurs rapidly according to the difference in amount between I_1 and I_2.	The behavior of the system is equivalent to that of an electronic switching circuit.		81

6	$I_1 \longrightarrow X_1 \xrightarrow{k_1} X_2 \xrightarrow{k_3}$ (cycle with A, B, k_{-1}, k_{-2}) $X_3 \longleftarrow I_2$ $k_4 \longleftarrow X_4 \xleftarrow{k_2} X_3$ Same assumptions as in model 3 except: The reactions $X_1 \rightarrow X_2$ and $X_3 \rightarrow X_4$ are reversible.	Increase in the values of the rate parameters, k_{-1} and k_{-2}, leads to a more gradual rise of $A(t)$ and $B(t)$, and the step function is not obtained. When the ratio of k_1/k_{-1} and k_2/k_{-2} is fixed at 1, increase in the rate parameters leads to a sharper rise of $A(t)$ and $B(t)$.	The system can be used as a switching controller when it is coupled to the reaction $S \rightarrow P$ and a cofactor A is essential to produce P. Thus, A can be controlled by I_1 and I_2 and the switch properties will be obtained for $P(t)$.
7	Same assumptions as in model 3 except: Reaction mechanisms are represented by ordered bi–bi enzymic kinetics. All reaction steps are assumed to be reversible.	The dynamic characteristics of $A(t)$ and $B(t)$ are qualitatively similar to those observed in model 3. The initial concentrations of the enzymes and cofactors affected the dynamic characteristics of the system significantly. The switch is obtained only when these concentrations are over a certain threshold value.	
8	Same assumptions as in model 1 except: Two sinusoidal inputs with a phase difference θ between them: $I_1(t) = 10 + 2\sin\left(\dfrac{2\pi}{40} t\right)$ $I_2(t) = 10 + 2\sin\left(\dfrac{2\pi}{40} t - \theta\right)$	The concentration profiles obtained for $A(t)$ and $B(t)$ show the switching observed in model 4, but the on/off times depend on θ. The frequency and amplitude of X_1 and X_3 depend on θ.	Focusing on the dynamics of $X_1(t)$ and $X_3(t)$, the system can play the role of a rectifier circuit. The amount of rectification depends on θ.

(continued)

Table 1.1 *(continued)*

Model No.	Model Characteristics	Conclusions and Applications	Results	Comments[a]	Refs.
9	Same assumptions as in model 4 except: Reaction mechanisms are represented by ordered bi–bi kinetics. All reaction steps assumed to be reversible.		As in model 4. Since the reaction involves several steps, the value of $A(t)$ or $B(t)$ when switched on was not the initial total concentration of them (1.0).		80
10	$I_1 \longrightarrow X_1 \xrightarrow{k_1} X_2 \xrightarrow{k_3}$; $B \xrightarrow{k_6} I_4$; $I_3 \xrightarrow{k_5} A$; $k_4 \longleftarrow X_4 \xleftarrow{k_2} X_3 \xleftarrow{} I_2$ I_1 and I_2 are represented by a sinusoidal function with time t. I_3 and I_4 are external inputs of A and B, respectively. k_5 and k_6 are degradation rate constants. $k_5 = k_6 = I_3(t) + I_4(t)$.		The switching time of the cyclic system can be regulated by I_3, I_4, as well as by I_1 and I_2. When a pulse of I_3 and I_4 is introduced, one can select the time of introduction in order for A or B to be switched-on thereafter. Introduction of I_3 or I_4 affect only the switching time of A and B, but not the oscillatory pattern of X_2 and X_4.	The comments concerning I_1 and I_2 are applicable to I_3 and I_4 as well.	83
11	C ; $I_1 \xrightarrow{k_1} X_1 \xrightarrow{k_2} X_2$; A , B ; $X_4 \xrightarrow{k_3} X_3 \xrightarrow{k_4} I_2$ Concentrations of I_1, I_2, X_2, and X_4 are held constant. C is the input parameter. All the reactions are reversible.	The system can act as a chemical neuron in which the concentration of A or B determines the state of the neuron (fire or quiescent).	A and B evolve in time to a unique steady state dictated by C. Steady-state concentrations of A and B show step functions in respect to C. k_2 and k_3 determine the steepness of the jump. When $k_2 \neq k_3$ the curves of the steady-state concentrations of A and B are not symmetric.	The mathematical equations for this model also agree with the case of batch reactions. Here the step $I_1 \rightarrow X_1$ is a catalytic reaction, and the step $I_2 \rightarrow X_3$ is a noncatalytic one.	109, 116

[a]These observations are those of the present authors.

10

Table 1.2 Models of Biochemical Networks Based on the Cyclic Enzyme System

Model No.	Model Characteristics	Results	Conclusions and Applications	Comments[a]	Refs.
1	 Coupled cyclic enzyme system: I_1 and I_2 are inputs to the system's pools of substrate X_1 and X_3, respectively; simple mass action kinetics; irreversible reactions.	A stepwise change in the steady-state concentration of $Y_i(t)$ is observed. The results are similar to those obtained using a monocyclic enzyme system (described in model 1 in Table 1.1).	The system can be applied for examination of control mechanisms of metabolic coupled enzyme systems, such as the sugar transport system in bacteria.	The mathematical equations for this model and for the following ones agree with the case of batch reactions, in which there is no mass flow into or out of the system. However, I_1 and I_2 cannot be defined as mass flows if volume changes are not considered.	79
2	 Bicyclic enzyme system: A, A′, B, and B′ are cofactors; I_1, I_2, and I_3 are constant inputs.	The steady-state concentrations of A and B ($\bar{A}$, $\bar{B}$) are determined by the minimum input among I_1, I_2 and I_3: I_1 minimum: $\bar{A}$, $\bar{B}$ = 0,1 I_2 minimum: $\bar{A}$, $\bar{B}$ = 1,1 I_3 minimum: $\bar{A}$, $\bar{B}$ = 1,0 I_1 and I_3 minimum: $\bar{A}$, $\bar{B}$ = 0,0	Based on the results presented, the basic logic functions NOT, AND, OR can be built using monocyclic or dicyclic enzyme systems.	The comments concerning I_1 and I_2 are applicable to I_3 as well.	81

(continued)

Table 1.2 (continued)

Model No.	Model Characteristics	Results	Conclusions and Applications	Comments[a]	Refs.
3		The number of excited elements in sequentially connected systems is related proportionally to the values of the excitatory stimulus. When the introduction of the excitatory stimulus is too late, it can not be transmitted. The excitatory stimulus is amplified to a certain limit and attenuated during propagation. By assuming several excitatory stimuli and varying their frequencies, the long-term potentiation phenomenon can be observed. Supposing reversible interactions between two elements, a continuous switching pattern of the output is observed.	One can interconnect basic elements excitatorially, inhibitorially, or reversibly and construct large networks.	The species A_i and A_j play the role of effector for another enzymic reaction, and their concentrations are not affected by this activity.	84,85

The basic element is similar to the one assumed in model 1 in Table 1.1. The jth element is assumed to have an excitatory or inhibitory affect on the ith element according to the following options:

(a) Excitatory interactions: A_i affects $X_{1,j}$

$$\frac{dX_{1,j}}{dt} = (I_{1,j} + W_i A_i) - k_{1,j} X_{1,j} B_j$$

(b) Inhibitory interactions: A_j affects $X_{3,i}$

$$\frac{dX_{3,i}}{dt} = (I_{2,i} + W_j A_j) - k_{2,i} X_{3,i} A_i$$

(c) Reversible interactions: both excitatory and inhibitory.

| 4 | External stimuli on a branched series of excitatory interactions, mentioned in model 3.

high-frequency input

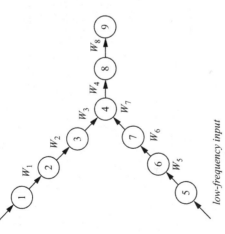

low-frequency input | High-frequency excitatory stimuli which were introduced to the first element was amplified and transmitted to the ninth element. Low-frequency excitatory stimuli which was introduced to the fifth element was attenuated during propagation leading to selective elimination of synaptic connection between the seventh and fourth elements. | The system shows the physiological phenomenon termed *selective elimination of synapses* generally produced as a result of a low-frequency train of electrical stimuli to the synapses. | 85 |

| 5 | External stimuli on a branched series of excitatory interactions, mentioned in models 3 and 4 except in the basic element the substrates $X_{1,i}$ and $X_{3,i}$ do not accumulate and are removed with k_5 and k_6 (model 5 in Table 1.1). | Selective elimination of synapses cannot be observed. | Neural network model composed of formal neurons without the capacity of memory storage cannot be applicable to the study of information processing of real neural networks. | |

(continued)

Table 1.2 *(continued)*

Model No.	Model Characteristics	Results	Conclusions and Applications	Comments[a]	Refs.
6					86

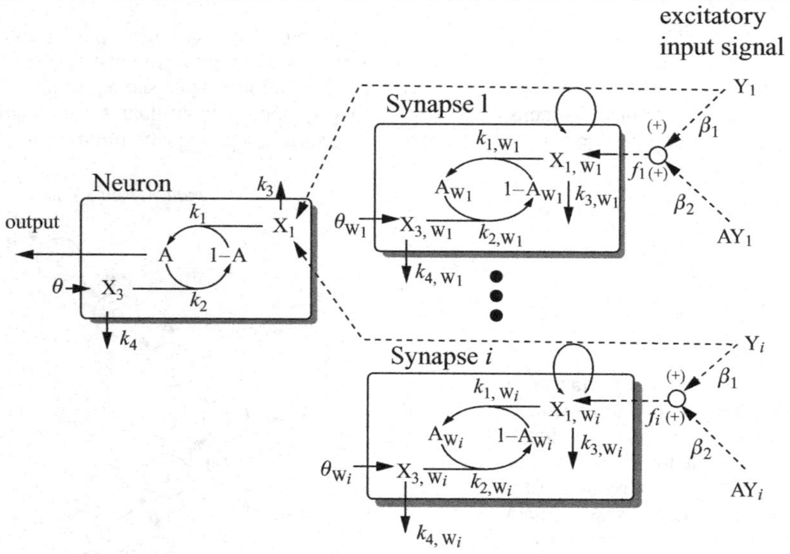

excitatory
input signal

Synapse 1

Synapse i

Neuron

output

X_{1,w_i}: synaptic efficacy for excitatory input Y_i at synapse i
$A(t)$: the output signal
θ: threshold value
β_1, β_2: arbitrary coefficients
f_i: feedback factor from output A
$f_i = (\beta_1 + \beta_2 A)Y_i$; $\quad i = 1, 2, \ldots, n$
$k_3, k_4 \gg k_{3,w_i}, k_{4,w_i}$

7

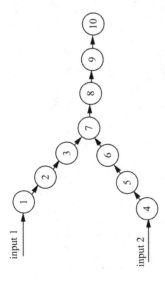

input 1

input 2

Each element is assumed to be composed of the basic scheme described in model 6, and to transmit the signal $A_i(t)$ to the subsequent one. When $0 < t < 60$, high-frequency input is introduced to the first element and low-frequency input is introduced to the fourth. When $60 < t < 120$, low-frequency input is introduced to the first element and high-frequency input is introduced to the fourth.

Excitatory high-frequency stimuli which were introduced to the first element during $0 < t < 60$ are amplified and transmitted successfully to the tenth element. Excitatory low-frequency stimuli which were introduced to the fourth element during $0 < t < 60$ are attenuated during propagation leading to selective elimination of synaptic connection. During $60 < t < 120$, excitatory high-frequency stimuli which were introduced to the fourth element turned out favorably, leading to the revival of the signal path from the fourth to the seventh, and the low-frequency stimuli introduced to the first element caused selective elimination of synaptic connection between the third and the seventh elements.

High-frequency activation of excitatory synapses produces a long-lasting increase in synaptic efficacy, and excitatory stimuli with low frequency are unfavorable for the growth of synaptic efficiency.

(continued)

Table 1.2 *(continued)*

Model No.	Model Characteristics	Results	Conclusions and Applications	Comments[a]	Refs.
8	Assumptions 1 to 6 as in model 6. The number of synapses denoted by i is 2. X_{1,w_1}, X_{1,w_2}: synaptic efficacies of the test path and conditioning path, respectively. Low-frequency test input and no conditioning input.	The test input itself has not caused long-term potentiation of the synaptic efficacy (X_{1,w_1} or X_{1,w_2}).			86
9	Assumptions 1 to 3 as in model 8. Low-frequency test input and high-frequency conditioning input are positively correlated. After the in-phase inputs are introduced 14 times only, the test input is reintroduced and the changes in X_{1,w_1} and A were investigated.	The synaptic efficacy X_{1,w_1} is potentiated during a long time period.			86
10	Assumptions 1 to 3 as in model 9. Low-frequency test input and high-frequency conditioning input are anticorrelated.	The synaptic efficacy X_{1,w_1} is weakened or depressed, leading to long-term depression of synaptic strength.			86

The biochemical neuron has another role as a "transducer" of external analog signals to impulse signals, where the external signals are received at the receptive field and transduced to impulse signals by cutting off at a certain threshold value.

The time courses of ExtIn(t) and $A_1(t)$ are almost the same except for the oscillatory behavior of $A_1(t)$. $A_0(t)$ behaves as a control variable which changes in value so as to minimize the function J:

$$J = \int_{t_0}^{t_f} [\text{ExtIn}(t) - A_1(t)]^2 \, dt$$

After the second layer the time courses of $A_i(t)$ are filtrated by the threshold value $\alpha_i/2$ and gradually settled to a two-state, having the values 0 and 1.0 only, and having a higher signal-to-noise ratio.

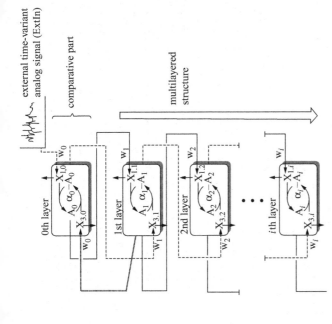

external time-variant analog signal (ExtIn)

comparative part

multilayered structure

0th layer 1st layer 2nd layer ith layer

α_i: threshold value for cutting off the signals. At the 0th layer, external analog signal ExtIn(t) and output of the first layer $A_1(t)$ are introduced to $X_{1,0}$ and $X_{3,0}$ respectively. Outputs of the $(i-1)$th layer, are the input of the ith layer. The external signal, ExtIn(t), is represented by a step function with time t:

$\alpha_i = 1, i = 0,1,2,\ldots,6.$

(continued)

Table 1.2 (continued)

Model No.	Model Characteristics	Results	Conclusions and Applications	Comments[a]	Refs.
12	Assumptions 1 to 3 as in model 11. The external analog signal, $\text{ExtIn}(t)$, has a uniform random value between 0 and 1. $\alpha_i = 1.8, i = 0,1,2,\ldots,5, \alpha_6 = 1.0.$	External random input signals are filtrated by the threshold value $\alpha_i/2 = 0.9$ and transformed into impulse signals.	By changing the α_i values, any time-variant external analog signal can be filtrated by an arbitrary threshold value.		86
13	 Each neuron is as in model 11 in Table 1.1. Neurons are chemically distinct. The effect of one neuron on the others is contained in C_i. Neuron i is affected by neurons j and k. A_j and B_j are activators of an enzyme $E_{i,j}$ to form $C_{i,j}$. The enzyme-activator reaction is fast and at equilibrium. A_j, A_k: inputs; C_i: output; $E_{i,j} \ll 1$ and $C_i = \sum_j C_{i,j}$.	For excitatory connections: $(E_{i,j} + A_j \rightleftharpoons C_{i,j})$: $C_{i,j} = \dfrac{E_{i,j}^0}{1 + \frac{k}{A_j}}$ For inhibitory connections: $(E_{i,j} + B_j \rightleftharpoons C_{i,j})$: $C_{i,j} = \dfrac{E_{i,j}^0}{1 + \frac{k}{k(A_0 - A_j)}}$ where k is the equilibrium constant. By adjusting the values of $E_{i,j}^0$ and k, neuron i can perform logic operations on the state of neurons j and k.	Various types of logic gates can be constructed when the threshold value for C_i is defined as 1: AND, OR, NOR, A_j AND NOT A_k.	Concentrations of A_i are set at $t = 0$ and the output is obtained at steady state. No time dependence is considered.	109

By changing the number of neurons, the form of the connections between them, and the definitions the concentrations that represent inputs and outputs to the system, various finite-state machines can be specified.

A binary decoder, a binary adder, and a stack memory can be built.

Assumptions 1 to 5 as in model 13. The state of the chemical neuron is allowed to change only at discrete times, dictated by an autonomously oscillating catalyst ε. The concentration of ε is very small except during short intervals. ε interacts with A_j or B_j of each neuron, and rapid equilibrium occurs when its concentration is large. $C_{i,j}$ can be activated/inhibited by more than one species:

$$E_i + A'_j \leftrightharpoons C_i$$
$$E_i + A'_k \leftrightharpoons (E_i A'_k)$$

---

[a]These observations are those of the present authors.

Table 1.3 Models of Other Biochemical Systems

Model No.	Model Characteristics	Results	Conclusions and Applications	Comments[a]	Refs.
1	E_a: active enzyme E_i: inactive enzyme x,y: excitatory and inhibitory factors, respectively; both factors remain constant during the reaction E_0: an enzyme with constant activity All the reactions are first order. Inputs: x and y; outputs: x_1 and x_2.	The steady-state concentrations of E_a and E_i show step functions with respect to the value of x/y: $E_a(x, y) = [0; x \geq y, 1; x < y]$ $E_i(x, y) = [1; x \geq y, 0; x < y]$ The concentrations of x_1 and x_2 change in a similar way except for the appearance of a curved corner whose magnitude seems to depend on the concentration of E_0.	The enzymic conjugate system described can realize the two-factor model. The system was included as a control element in a feedback system. In this case, a specific configuration of the control element can maintain the value of the end product at a desired level.		76
2	$A* \xrightarrow{E_1} B \longrightarrow P*$ The concentrations of A and P are held constant. The conversion of B to P follows Michaelis–Menten kinetics. I_1 and I_2: two external effectors of E_1 Output: steady-state concentration of B Input: concentration of I_1 and I_2.	Three different mechanisms for the kinetics of E_1 can be used to construct three different logic gates: AND, OR, and XOR. The degree of cooperativity in the binding of E_1 and I_1 or I_2 determines the steepness of the transition from low to high steady-state concentrations of B.			115

3

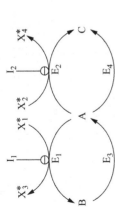

E_1 to E_4 are irreversible enzymes that follow Michaelis–Menten kinetics. E_1 and E_2 are inhibited by the noncompetitive inhibitors I_1 and I_2. Concentrations of X_i are held constant. Inputs: concentrations of I_1 and I_2. Output: steady-state concentration of A. The concentrations of the species marked with (*) are fixed.

When no inhibitors are present, the steady-state concentrations of A, B, and C are equivalent. When one of the inhibitors is present, the material is apportioned between A and one of the other species. When both inhibitors are present, conversion of A to the other species is blocked. The steepness of transition between the highest and lowest concentrations of A, the values of these concentrations, and the symmetry of the response depend on the kinetic parameters of the enzymes.

The system can function as a logical AND gate.

4

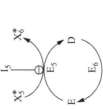

E_5 and E_6 are irreversible enzymes that follow Michaelis–Menten kinetics. E_5 is inhibited by the noncompetitive inhibitor I_5. Concentrations of X_i are held constant. Inputs: concentrations of I_5. Output: steady-state concentration of D. The concentrations of the species marked with (*) are fixed.

The concentration of D is high (low) when the concentration of I_5 is low (high). The steepness of transition between the highest and lowest concentrations of D and the value of this concentration depend on the kinetic parameters of the enzymes.

The system can function as a logical NOT gate.

(continued)

Table 1.3 *(continued)*

Model No.	Model Characteristics	Results	Conclusions and Applications	Comments[a]	Refs.
5	 Three NOT gates (model 4), and one AND gate (model 3). Inputs: concentrations of I_1 and I_2. Output: steady-state concentration of D_3.	The output reaches its maximum value when one of the inputs or both of them are present in significant amounts. The output is minimized when neither input chemical is present.	The system can function as a logical OR gate.		115

[a]The observations are those of the present authors.

The works presented in Tables 1.1 to 1.3 [76–86,109–122] deal only with theoretical aspects of the enzymic biochemical devices, and the biochemical devices were not carried into practice. Moreover, Okamoto [85] suggests using silicon technology instead of biomaterials for practical implementation of the device based on the cyclic enzyme system.

This study is also based on the cyclic enzyme system, but its leading concept is to accomplish practical implementation of this system using biomaterials. In this respect, the analytical models developed here are related to several biochemical reactors in which enzymic reactions take place. This practical approach cannot be found in the models reviewed [76–86,109–122].

1.5   OSCILLATIONS IN BIOCHEMICAL SYSTEMS

Many oscillatory patterns can be found in biological systems [123–126]. It is generally recognized in engineering that encoding information in a frequency provides resistance to degradation by noise and enhanced precision of control. Rapp [124] suggested that many biological oscillations can be envisaged to reflect the biochemical implementation of this control strategy.

Intracellular communication often proceeds in a pulsatile, rhythmic manner [126]. Moreover, an increasing number of hormones are found to be secreted in a pulsatile manner, and the physiological efficiency of these signals appears to be closely related to their frequency [126]. Based on this understanding, a number of classes of drug therapies have been shown to require a periodic, pulsatile regimen of delivery for efficacy or optimization [131], and several delivery strategies have been proposed to respond to this need [127–131].

1.6   KINETIC CHARACTERISTICS OF CYCLIC ENZYME SYSTEMS

Many examples of enzymatic cyclic systems have been developed in practice [87–107]. These systems can be utilized to construct the biochemical device proposed by Okamoto et al. [76–86]. The kinetic properties of five enzymes that catalyze reactions in which cofactors are required, and therefore can participate in a cyclic enzyme system, are summarized in Table 1.4 [132–144]. These enzymes are glucose-6-phosphate dehydrogenase (G6PDH, E.C. 1.1.1.49), glutathione reductase (GR, E.C. 1.6.4.2), glucose dehydrogenase (GDH, E.C. 1.1.1.47), L-lactate dehydrogenase (LDH, E.C. 1.1.1.27), and alcohol dehydrogenase (ADH, E.C. 1.1.1.1).

Table 1.4 Kinetic Properties of Enzymes Used in Cyclic Systems

Enzyme	Process	K_m values	Reaction Mechanism	Conditions	Other Findings	Refs.
G6PDH From brewer's yeast	Glucose-6-phosphate + NADP → gluconate-6-phosphate + NADPH	$K_{m,G6P} = 6.9 \times 10^{-5}$ M $K_{m,NADP} = 3.3 \times 10^{-5}$ M In the presence of MgCl$_2$ 0.01 M: $K_{m,G6P} = 5.8 \times 10^{-5}$ M $K_{m,NADP} = 2.0 \times 10^{-5}$ M		0.063 M Tris buffer, pH 8 at 25°C	The enzyme is inhibited by NADPH, which is competitive with NADP. The inhibition constant $K_i = 2.7 \times 10^{-5}$ M. The reaction is reversible and the equilibrium constant is $6 \pm 0.7 \times 10^{-7}$ M at 28°C.	132
From *Candida utilis*		$K_{m,G6P} = 2.3 \times 10^{-4}$ M $K_{m,NADP} = 6.7 \times 10^{-5}$ M		93 mM glycine–NaOH buffer pH 9.1, also containing 9.3 mM MgCl$_2$ and 0.93 mM EDTA		133
GR From baker's yeast	Oxidized glutathione + NADPH → reduced glutathione + NADP	$K_{m,GSSG} = 6.1 \times 10^{-5}$ M $K_{m,NADPH} = 7.6 \times 10^{-6}$ M		Phosphate buffer, pH 7.6 at 25°C		134
From sea urchin egg		$K_{m,GSSG} = 1 \times 10^{-4}$ M $K_{m,NADPH} = 5 \times 10^{-6}$ M		0.1 M potassium–phosphate buffer, pH 7.2, containing 1 mM EDTA	Addition of 1 mM EDTA increases the enzyme activity. Further addition of EDTA shows no further effect.	135

GDH From beef liver	Glucose + NAD $\rightarrow$ glucono-δ-lactone + NADH	$K_{m,\text{NAD}} = 4.3 \times 10^{-6}$ M pH $\quad K_{m,\text{glucose}}$ (M) 6.28 $\quad 34.9 \times 10^{-2}$ 7.00 $\quad 3.13 \times 10^{-2}$ 8.92 $\quad 32.6 \times 10^{-2}$	0.05 M phosphate buffer, pH 7.6 at 21–22°C	The reaction is reversible and the equilibrium constant is 2.9–3.3 $\times 10^{-7}$ M.	136
From ox liver		$K_{m,\text{glucose}} = 15 \times 10^{-2}$ M $K_{m,\text{NAD}} = 1.5 \times 10^{-5}$ M $K_{m,\text{glucose}} = 7 \times 10^{-2}$ M	0.05 M phosphate buffer, pH 7 0.05 M phosphate buffer, pH 7.6	The reaction is reversible and the equilibrium constant is 30 $\times 10^{-7}$ M at pH 7.	137 138
From rat liver		$K_{m,\text{glucose}} = 0.3$–0.7 M $K_{m,\text{NAD}} = 0.38\ \mu$M $K_{m,\text{NADP}} = 0.45\ \mu$M	Phosphate buffer, pH 8.2		
From *Bacillus Megaterium*		$K_{m,\text{glucose}} = 47.5 \times 10^{-3}$ M $K_{m,\text{NAD}} = 4.5 \times 10^{-3}$ M $K_{i,\text{NAD}} = 69 \times 10^{-5}$ M	Acetate–borate buffer, pH 9 at 25°C	Ordered Bi–Bi	139
LDH From rabbit muscle	Pyruvate + NADH $\rightarrow$ lactate + NAD	$K_{m,\text{pyruvate}} = 5.2 \times 10^{-5}$ M			140

(continued)

Table 1.4 Kinetic Properties of Enzymes Used in Cyclic Systems (*continued*)

Enzyme	Process	K_m values	Conditions	Reaction Mechanism	Other Findings	Refs.
LDH From rabbit muscle	Pyruvate + NADH → Lactate + NAD	$K_{m,\text{pyruvate}} = 15 \times 10^{-6}$ M $K_{m,\text{NADH}} = 35 \times 10^{-7}$ M $K_{\text{PN}} = 6.5 \times 10^{-12}$ M²	0.05 M sodium phosphate buffer, pH 6.8 at 25°C	Ordered Bi-Bi. $$\frac{V_m}{V} = 1 + \frac{K_{m,P}}{[P]} + \frac{K_{m,N}}{[\text{NADH}]} + \frac{K_{\text{PN}}}{[P][\text{NADH}]}$$	The reaction is reversible and the equilibrium constant is 2.76 × 10⁻¹² M at pH 7 and 25°C. Pyruvate is an inhibitor.	141
		$K_{m,\text{pyruvate}} = 1.64 \times 10^{-4}$ M $K_{m,\text{NADH}} = 1.07 \times 10^{-5}$ M $K_{\text{PN}} = 1.38 \times 10^{-9}$ M²	0.25 M phosphate buffer, pH 6.8 at 25°C		Pyruvate and lactate inhibit the enzyme with $K_{I,\text{pyruvate}} = 2.02 \times 10^{-4}$ M $K_{I,\text{lactate}} = 0.209$ M	142
From *Lactobacillus plantarum*	Pyruvate + NADH → lactate + NAD	$K_{m,\text{pyruvate}} = 3.7 \times 10^{-4}$ M	0.1 M Tris buffer, pH 8			143
ADH From baker's yeast	Ethanol + NAD → acetaldehyde + NADH	pH / $K_{m,\text{NAD}}$ (mM) / $K_{m,\text{Eth.}}$ (mM) / $K_{i,\text{NAD}}$ (mM): 4.9, 0.224, 107, 0.390; 5.95, 0.106, 43, 0.340; 7.05, 0.108, 26, 0.270; 8.1, 0.118, 18.5, 0.385; 8.9, 0.150, 10, 0.860; 9.9, 0.200, 5, 2.40	0.01 M acetic acid–sodium acetate buffer, pH 4.9; 0.1 M phosphate buffer, pH 5.95, 7.05, 8.1; 0.01 M glycine-NaOH buffer, pH 8.9, 9.9	Ordered Bi–Bi	The reaction is reversible and the equilibrium constant is 0.98 × 10⁻¹¹ M at 25°C	144

2

BACKGROUND AND GOALS OF THIS STUDY

Living organisms and computers share the common characteristic of being information-processing machines which operate according to well-defined programs. However, in their operation the two entities also differ from one another. Thus, internal production and assembly of composing elements take place in living organisms but not in artificial machines. Moreover, the operational rules governing the function of the two entities are built into the living organisms but are provided from the outside for artificial computers. These similarities and differences have drawn the attention of computer scientists and of life scientists as well.

Aims of the Study

Biochemical systems have the advantage of using the "language" of the physiological processes: the biochemical reactions. As such, they can be organized into the neural network–type assemblies in much the way that natural biosystems are. This book is concerned with well-delineated biochemical assemblies and is directed at assessing their ability to perform information-processing operations. In particular, this book is intended :

1. To examine the cyclic enzyme system proposed by Okamoto et al. [76–86] as an information-processing unit when this model is implemented in an experimental system and the enzymic reactions take place

Information Processing by Biochemical Systems: Neural Network–Type Configurations, By Orna Filo and Noah Lotan
Copyright © 2010 John Wiley & Sons, Inc.

in a biochemical reactor (of fed-batch, continuous stirred tank, or packed bed type).

2. To expand the cyclic enzyme system and control the enzymic reaction with the use of an external inhibitor, and to examine the characteristics of this new system as an information-processing unit.

3. To develop analytical models that describe the performance of a cyclic enzyme system (herein termed the *basic system*) and a cyclic enzyme system with an external inhibitor (termed the *extended basic system*) when operated in different modes: as a fed-batch reactor or a continuous reactor. These models enable us to design systems and select operational conditions according to needs.

4. To connect several basic systems into a biochemical network and examine the performance of various networks as a function of the connectivity between the basic systems and their operational parameters. To this end, analytical models for each network type will be developed.

5. To reveal the similarities and differences between the biochemical networks developed in this study and artificial neural networks described in the literature.

6. To implement the principles of the basic system and extended basic systems into experimental systems operated in several operational modes. The analytical models developed in this study will be used to design experimental operational conditions and to investigate the results obtained.

Results

The basic system considered in this study relies on well-defined enzymic reactions and is designed to function as a "node" or "biochemical neuron" in biochemical networks. This system involves two enzyme-catalyzed reactions, coupled to one another by the use of a cofactor, the latter being cycled continuously between the two. In addition, the two consumable substrates are fed into the system continuously at predetermined concentrations and rates. Also considered in this work was an extension of the *basic system* termed the *extended basic system*. The extended system relies on the same reactions as those in the basic system; in addition, an external compound, inhibitory to one of the enzymes, is fed into the system.

The research was carried out on two main avenues. The first is a theoretical investigation in which analytical models were developed and their characteristics were studied by numerical simulations; the second is experimental research in which systems designed and studied in the former part of the program were implemented as biochemical reactors. In the first stage of the research, analytical models were developed for both the basic system and the extended basic system. These models consider that the reactions take place in an enzymic reactor. For each reaction an expression for the instantaneous rate was written that correlates the maximum reaction rate, the concentrations of the substrates, and the pertinent Michaelis constants, as well as the concentration of the products and their characteristic inhibition constants.

Subsequently, analytical expressions for the time dependence concentration of all components in the system were obtained based on mass balance principles and also considering the reactor type, the flow rates of the feed streams, and the concentrations of substrates. Using these models we found that the basic system considered is able to perform several information-processing functions, such as division, rectification, and switching.

In the second stage of the research, a higher level of organization of the biosystems was considered. To this aim, the basic system presented above was used to construct biochemical networks. This was achieved by connecting a number of basic systems according to the principles of neural networks. This part of the research allowed us to delineate the rules for connecting the basic systems into functional biochemical networks and to study the type of information processing that can be achieved in a defined network.

In support of the theoretical investigations mentioned above, pertinent experimental studies were also carried out. The experimental basic system considered is driven by the concerted action of two enzymes: glucose-6-phosphate dehydrogenase and glutathione reductase. In this system glucose-6-phosphate and oxidized glutathione were used as the consumable substrates, with NADP and NADPH serving as the coupling cofactors. The basic system was operated in two modes: a fed-batch reactor where soluble enzymes were employed, and a packed bed reactor in which immobilized enzymes were employed. The experimental extended basic system involved the same components as those in the basic system, with the addition of D-glucosamine-6-phosphate, which acts as an inhibitor to the enzyme glucose-6-phosphate dehydrogenase. The extended basic system was operated in a packed bed reactor with immobilized enzymes.

Conclusions

The results obtained from the experimental studies confirm that the information-processing functions predicted by the pertinent analytical models can be achieved experimentally. Moreover, these results support the view that artificial biochemical neurons can be implemented in practice for information-processing purposes. Furthermore, because of the very high dependence of the system function on the internal parameters and the relations between them, the analytical models developed are essential tools for the engineering design of such systems as well as for determination of the operational parameters required for these systems to perform the information-processing function desired.

3

MATERIALS AND METHODS

3.1 MATERIALS

Enzymes

- Glucose-6-phosphate dehydrogenase (from *Torula* yeast) suspension
  Activity: 520 Units/mg protein, Sigma (Lot 13H80602), USA
- Glutathione reductase (from baker's yeast)
  Activity: 200 Units/mg protein, Sigma (Lot 121H80701), USA
- Glucose dehydrogenase (from *Bacillus megaterium*)
  Activity: 131 Units/mg protein, Sigma (Lot 83H1010), USA
- L-Lactic dehydrogenase (from rabbit muscle) suspension
  Activity: 950 Units/mg protein, Sigma (Lot 92H9555), USA
- Alcohol dehydrogenase (from baker's yeast)
  Activity: 360 Units/mg protein, Sigma (Lot 33H8006), USA

Information Processing by Biochemical Systems: Neural Network–Type Configurations, By Orna Filo and Noah Lotan
Copyright © 2010 John Wiley & Sons, Inc.

Substrates

- D-Glucose-6-phosphate, Sigma (Lot 51F3826), USA

$$
\begin{array}{c}
\quad\quad\ O \\
\quad\quad\ \| \\
O - P - O \\
\quad\quad\ | \\
\quad\quad\ O
\end{array}
$$

- Pyruvic acid, Merck (Lot 9155268), Germany

$$
H_3C - \overset{\overset{\displaystyle O}{\|}}{C} - \overset{\overset{\displaystyle O}{\|}}{C} - OH
$$

- Ethyl alcohol (absolute), Fluka, Switzerland

$H_3C{-}CH_2OH$

- Glutathione (oxidized form), Sigma (Lot 80H82151), USA

Cofactors

- β-Nicotinamide adenine dinucleotide (β-NAD), Sigma (Lot 123H7821), USA

- β-Nicotinamide adenine dinucleotide, reduced form (β-NADH), Sigma (Lot 103H78062), USA

- β-Nicotinamide adenine dinucleotide phosphate (β-NADP), Sigma (Lot 73H7879), USA

- β-Nicotinamide adenine dinucleotide phosphate, reduced form (β-NADPH), Sigma (Lot 74H7081), USA

Inhibitor

- D-Glucosamine-6-phosphate, Sigma (Lot 104H7095), USA

$$
\begin{array}{c}
\overset{\displaystyle O}{\underset{\displaystyle |}{\overset{\displaystyle \|}{}}} \\
O - P - O \\
| \\
O \\
| \\
H_2C
\end{array}
$$

HO — ⟨ring⟩ — OH (O)

HO   NH$_2$

Enzyme Support

- Affi-Gel 10, Bio-Rad (Lot 47624A), USA.

Others

- Ethylenediaminetetraacetic acid (EDTA), Fluka, Switzerland
- Magnesium chloride hexahydrate, Merck, Germany

All other materials used were of analytical grade.

3.2   INSTRUMENTS

- Peristaltic pumps, Model P-1, Pharmacia, Sweden
- Column, Model C10/20, Pharmacia, Sweden
- Spectrophotometer, Spectronic 2000, Bausch and Lomb, USA
- Spectrophotometer, HP 8452A diode array, Hewlett-Packard, USA
- Data acquisition board, DT 2811-PGH, Data Translation Inc., USA
- Interface DT2811
- Pump controller

3.3   EXPERIMENTAL METHODS

3.3.1   Determination of Kinetic Constants

Kinetic parameters for two substrate reactions were determined by measuring the initial reaction rates as a function of the concentration of one of the substrates, at constant concentration of the second substrate. Experimental data were analyzed using Lineweaver–Burk reciprocal plots [146] and taking into account the particular mechanism of the reaction considered.

3.3.1.1   Kinetic Constants for a Reaction Catalyzed by Glucose Dehydrogenase

The reaction considered is

$$\beta\text{-D-glucose} + \text{NAD} \rightarrow \text{D-glucono-}\delta\text{-lactone} + \text{NADH}$$

Determination of the Michaelis constant for the cofactor NAD ($K_{m,\text{NAD}}$) was carried out by measuring the initial rate of the reduction of NAD as a function of its concentration, at a constant concentration of glucose. All solutions were prepared in 0.1 M phosphate buffer pH 7.55.

The reaction mixture contained:

- 2 mL of 0.87 M glucose solution
- 10 μL of enzyme solution (1.4 mg GDH in 1 mL phosphate buffer)
- 0.5 mL of NAD solution (five different solution concentrations between 0.215 and 2.15 mM)

The increase in absorption at 339 nm was measured for 5 min. From the experimental data, the reciprocal plot ($1/V$ versus $1/[\text{NAD}]$) was obtained. In this case, glucose was present at a saturating concentration. Therefore, data were interpreted in terms of the basic Michaelis–Menten formalism.

Determination of the Michaelis constant for glucose ($K_{m,\text{glucose}}$) was carried out by measuring the initial rate of reduction of NAD as a function of glucose concentration at a constant concentration of NAD. All solutions were prepared in 0.1 M phosphate buffer pH 7.55.

The reaction mixture contained:

- 2 mL of 2.15 mM NAD solution
- 10 μL of enzyme solution (1.4 mg of GDH in 1 mL phosphate buffer)
- 0.5 mL of glucose solution (five different solution concentrations between 87.12 and 3.5 mM)

The increase in absorption at 339 nm was measured for 5 min. From the experimental data, the reciprocal plot ($1/V$ versus $1/[\text{glucose}]$) was obtained. In this case, NAD was not present at a saturating concentration. Therefore, data were interpreted in terms of the kinetic equation for the Ordered Bi–Bi mechanism [139].

3.3.1.2   Kinetic Constants for a Reaction Catalyzed
by Lactate Dehydrogenase

The reaction considered is

$$\text{pyruvate} + \text{NADH} \rightarrow \text{L-lactate} + \text{NAD}$$

Determination of the Michaelis constant for the cofactor NADH ($K_{m,\text{NADH}}$) was carried out by measuring the initial rate of oxidation of NADH as a function of its concentration, at a constant concentration of pyruvate. All the solutions were prepared in 0.1 M phosphate buffer pH 7.55.

The reaction mixture contained:

- 2 mL of 7.2 mM pyruvate solution
- 10 μL of enzyme solution (1 μl LDH in 5 mL phosphate buffer)
- 0.5 mL of NADH solution (five different solution concentrations between 0.0146 and 0.146 mM)

The decrease in absorption at 339 nm was measured for 5 min. From the experimental data, the reciprocal plot ($1/V$ versus $1/[\text{NADH}]$) was obtained. In this case, pyruvate was present at saturating concentration. Therefore, data were interpreted in terms of the basic Michaelis–Menten formalism.

Determination of the Michaelis constant for pyruvate ($K_{m,\text{pyruvate}}$) was carried out by measuring the initial rate of oxidation of NADH as a function of pyruvate concentration at a constant concentration of NADH. All the solutions were prepared in 0.1 M phosphate buffer pH 7.55.

The reaction mixture contained:

- 0.5 mL of 1.46 mM NADH solution
- 10 μL of enzyme solution (10 μL LDH in 1 mL phosphate buffer)
- 2 mL of pyruvate solution (six different solution concentrations between 0.018 and 0.18 mM)

The decrease in absorption at 339 nm was measured for 5 min. From the experimental data, the reciprocal plot ($1/V$ versus $1/[\text{pyruvate}]$) was obtained. In this case, NADH was not present at saturating concentration. Therefore, data were interpreted in terms of the kinetic equation for the Ordered Bi–Bi mechanism [141,142].

3.3.1.3   Kinetic Constants for a Reaction Catalyzed
by Alcohol Dehydrogenase

The reaction considered is

$$\text{ethanol} + \text{NAD} \rightarrow \text{acetaldehyde} + \text{NADH}$$

Determination of the Michaelis constant for the cofactor NAD ($K_{m,NAD}$) was carried out by measuring the initial rate of the reduction of NAD as a function of its concentration at a constant concentration of ethanol. All the solutions were prepared in 0.1 M phosphate buffer pH 7.55.

The reaction mixture contained:

- 30 μL of ethanol (absolute)
- 10 μL of enzyme solution (48 mg ADH in 4.6 mL phosphate buffer)
- 2 mL of NAD solution (four different solution concentrations between 0.13 and 0.65 mM)

The increase in absorption at 339 nm was measured for 5 min. From the experimental data, the reciprocal plot ($1/V$ versus $1/$[NAD]) was obtained. In this case, ethanol was present at a saturating concentration. Therefore, data were interpreted in terms of the basic Michaelis–Menten formalism.

Determination of the Michaelis constant for ethanol ($K_{m,ethanol}$) was carried out by measuring the initial rate of reduction of NAD as a function of ethanol concentration at a constant concentration of NAD. All the solutions were prepared in 0.1 M phosphate buffer pH 7.55.

The reaction mixture contained:

- 2 mL of 2.61 mM NAD solution
- 10 μL of enzyme solution (48 mg ADH in 4.6 mL phosphate buffer)
- 30 μL of ethanol solution (five different solution concentrations between 17.15 and 0.57 M)

The increase in absorption at 339 nm was measured for 5 min. From the experimental data, the reciprocal plot ($1/V$ versus $1/$[ethanol]) was obtained. In this case, NAD was not present at a saturating concentration. Therefore, data were interpreted in terms of the kinetic equation for the Ordered Bi–Bi mechanism [144].

3.3.1.4 Reaction Mechanism and Kinetic Constants for a Reaction Catalyzed by Glucose-6-Phosphate Dehydrogenase

The reaction considered is

D-glucose-6-phosphate + NADP → D-gluconate-6-phosphate + NADPH

Determination of the reaction mechanism and the Michaelis constants for G6P ($K_{m,G6P}$) and the cofactor NADP ($K_{m,NADP}$) was carried out by measuring the initial rate of the reduction of NADP at various concentrations of G6P. This procedure was repeated five times with another concentration of NADP employed each time. All the solutions were prepeared in 0.1 M Tris buffer pH 8 containing 10 mM $MgCl_2$ and 0.94 mM EDTA.

The reaction mixture contained:

- 1 mL of NADP solution (a separate solution concentration for each experiment: 1.25 mM, 0.63 mM, 0.31 mM, 0.19 mM, 0.125 mM)
- 10 μL of enzyme solution (60 μL of G6PDH in 1 mL of Tris buffer)
- 2 mL of G6P solution (five different solution concentrations between 1.86 and 0.23 mM)

The increase in absorption at 339 nm was measured for 5 min. From the experimental data, reciprocal plots (1/V versus 1/[G6P] at various concentrations of NADP) were obtained. A detailed analysis is given in Section 4.3.2.1.

3.3.1.5   Reaction Mechanism and Kinetic Constants for a Reaction Catalyzed by Glutathione Reductase

The reaction considered is

glutathione (oxidized) + NADPH $\rightarrow$ glutathione (reduced) + NADP

Determination of the reaction mechanism and the Michaelis constants for GSSG ($K_{m,GSSG}$) and the cofactor NADPH ($K_{m,NADPH}$) was carried out by measuring the initial rate of the oxidation of NADPH at various concentrations of GSSG. This procedure was repeated four times with another concentration of NADPH employed each time. All the solutions were prepared in 0.1 M Tris buffer pH 8 containing 10 mM $MgCl_2$ and 0.94 mM EDTA.

The reaction mixture contained:

- 1 mL of NADPH solution (a separate solution concentration for each experiment: 0.43 mM, 0.29 mM, 0.14 mM, 0.07 mM)
- 10 μL of enzyme solution (20 μL of G6PDH in 1 mL of Tris buffer)
- 2 mL of GSSG solution (five different solution concentrations between 0.11 and 2.21 mM)

The decrease in absorption at 339 nm was measured for 5 min. From the experimental data, reciprocal plots (1/V versus 1/[GSSG] at various concentrations of NADPH) were obtained. A detailed analysis is given in Section 4.3.2.2.

3.3.2 Determination of the Inhibition Constant for Inhibition of Glutathione Reductase by Glucose-6-Phosphate

The inhibition constant for the process in which the enzyme glutathione reductase is inhibited by G6P was determined by measuring the initial rate of the oxidation of NADPH at various concentrations of GSSG. This procedure was repeated four times, each time with a separate concentration of the inhibitor G6P. All the solutions were prepeared in 0.1 M Tris buffer pH 8 containing 10 mM $MgCl_2$ and 0.94 mM EDTA.

The reaction mixture contained:

- 0.2 mL of 1.28 mM NADPH solution
- 10 μL of enzyme solution (20 μL G6PDH in 1 mL of Tris buffer)
- 1 mL of GSSG solution (five different solution concentrations between 0.22 and 4.43 mM)
- 2 mL of G6P solution (a separate solution concentration for each experiment: 0, 30 mM, 60.2 mM, 120 mM)

The decrease in absorption at 339 nm was measured for 5 min. From the experimental data, reciprocal plots ($1/V$ versus $1/[GSSG]$ at various concentrations of G6P) were obtained. The detailed analysis is given in Section 4.3.5.

3.3.3 Immobilization on Affi-Gel 10

Immobilization of the enzymes GR and G6PDH was carried out by coupling them to Affi-Gel 10 support. Affi-Gel 10 is an N-hydroxysuccinimide ester of a derivatized cross-linked agarose gel. Upon addition of the enzyme to Affi-Gel 10, the N-hydroxysuccinimide is displaced and the free amino groups of the enzyme form a stable amide bond with the gel. The enzymes GR and G6PDH were immobilized separately following the procedure described below.

Five milliliters of Aff-Gel 10 were transfered to a Buchner funnel and washed with 20 mL of cold (4°C) 0.01 M sodium acetate pH 4.5. The washed gel was transferred to a flask and the enzyme solution was added (0.2 mg of enzyme in 2.5 mL of 0.1 M Hepes buffer pH 7). The suspension was agitated gently on a wheel for 1 h at room temperature or 24 h at 4°C. Blocking of remaining active esters was accomplished by adding 0.5 mL of 1 M ethanolamine HCl pH 8 to the suspension and agitating for 1 h. The gel was transferred to a column and washed with 0.1 M Tris buffer pH 8 until it was free of reactants, as detected by OD_{280} (optical density at 280 nm). The gel was stored at 4°C.

3.3.4   Assay of Glucose-6-Phosphate Dehydrogenase

3.3.4.1   Assay of Soluble Glucose-6-Phosphate Dehydrogenase

The reaction mixture contained:

- 1.5 mL of 3.4 mM G6P solution
- 1.5 mL of 1.6 mM NADP solution
- 10 μL of enzyme solution

All the solutions were prepared in 0.1 M Tris buffer pH 8 containing 10 mM $MgCl_2$ and 0.94 mM EDTA. The increase in absorption at 339 nm was measured for 5 min, and a unit of G6PDH is defined as the amount of enzyme that will yield 1 μmol of NADPH per minute.

3.3.4.2   Assay of Immobilized Glucose-6-Phosphate Dehydrogenase

The reaction mixture contained:

- 1.5 mL of 3.4 mM G6P solution
- 1.5 mL of 1.6 mM NADP solution
- 100 μL of the gel containing the enzyme

All the solutions were prepared in 0.1 M Tris buffer pH 8 containing 10 mM $MgCl_2$ and 0.94 mM EDTA. The increase in absorption at 339 nm was measured for 5 min, and a unit of immobilized G6PDH is defined as the amount of enzyme that will yield 1 μmol of NADPH per minute.

3.3.5   Assay of Glutathione Reductase

3.3.5.1   Assay of Soluble Glutathione Reductase

The reaction mixture contained:

- 1.5 mL of 1 mM glutathione (oxidized) solution
- 1.5 mL of 0.44 mM NADPH solution
- 10 μL of enzyme solution

All the solutions were prepared in 0.1 M Tris buffer pH 8 containing 10 mM $MgCl_2$ and 0.94 mM EDTA. The decrease in absorption at 339 nm was measured for 5 min, and a unit of GR is defined as the amount of enzyme that will yield 1 μmol of NADP per minute.

3.3.5.2   *Assay of Immobilized Glutathione Reductase*

The reaction mixture contained:

- 1.5 mL of 1 mM glutathione (oxidized) solution
- 1.5 mL of 0.44 mM NADPH solution
- 100 μL of the gel containing the enzyme

All the solutions were prepeared in 0.1 M Tris buffer pH 8 containing 10 mM $MgCl_2$ and 0.94 mM EDTA. The decrease in absorption at 339 nm was measured for 5 min, and a unit of immobilized GR is defined as the amount of enzyme that will yield 1 μmol of NADP per minute.

3.4   COMPUTATIONAL METHODS

For each system considered, an appropriate computer program was written for solving the equations involved in the modeling presented in Section 4.1. The first-order nonlinear differential equations were solved by numerical integration using the Runge–Kutta procedure [141].

4

RESULTS

4.1 THE BASIC SYSTEM: THEORETICAL CONSIDERATIONS AND RESULTS

The system presented below [76–86] relies on well-defined enzymic reactions and is termed the basic system. This system was designed to function as an information-processing unit and is defined and characterized in Section 4.1.1. Its characteristics as an information-processing unit are described in Section 4.1.2. In Section 4.1.3 the analytical models written for various operational modes of the basic system are presented. Using these models, numerical simulations were carried out, and their results are presented in Section 4.1.4.

4.1.1 Characteristics of the Basic System

The basic system considered here relies on well-defined enzymic reactions. This system is shown in Figure 4.1 and involves two enzyme-catalyzed reactions:

$$S_1 + A \rightarrow P_1 + B \qquad \text{reaction (1)} \tag{1}$$

$$S_2 + B \rightarrow P_2 + A \qquad \text{reaction (2)} \tag{2}$$

These reactions are coupled to one another by the cofactors A and B, which are cycled continuously between them. In addition, the two consumable

---

Information Processing by Biochemical Systems: Neural Network–Type Configurations, By Orna Filo and Noah Lotan
Copyright © 2010 John Wiley & Sons, Inc.

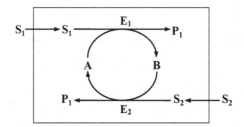

Figure 4.1   Basic system. S_1, S_2: substrates; P_1, P_2: products; E_1, E_2: participating enzymes.

substrates, S_1 and S_2, are fed into the system continuously at predetermined concentrations ($[S_1]_0$, $[S_2]_0$) and rates.

4.1.2   The Basic System as an Information-Processing Unit

The basic system is designed to function as an information-processing unit that receives an input signal, processes it through a specific function, and produces the output signal.

a. Input   In the basic system described here (Figure 4.1) the input signal is composed of the concentration profiles of substrates S_1 and S_2 in the feed streams entering the system. The concentration profiles used in this study are shown in Figure 4.2. Several parameters are used here to define the input signal (Figure 4.2):

- *Cycle time (τ):* the time required for changing the concentration of a given substrate in the feed stream from the minimum value to the maximum value, or the other way around.

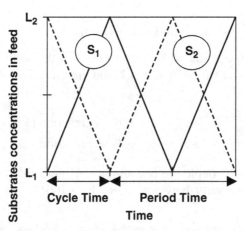

Figure 4.2   Input signal to the basic system. (—): $[S_1]_0$; (− −):$[S_2]_0$.

- **Time period (π):** the time between two adjacent minimum or maximum values of $[S_1]_0$ and $[S_2]_0$ (i.e., $\pi = 2\tau$).
- **Range:** the minimum and maximum values of $[S_1]_0$ and $[S_2]_0$ (i.e., L_1 and L_2, respectively).
- **Amplitude:** the difference between the minimum and maximum values of $[S_1]_0$ and $[S_2]_0$ (i.e., $L_2 - L_1$).

b. Processing Function   This is defined as the enzymic reactions taking place in the basic system and is determined by the parameters of the enzymic reactions and the operational system. This dependence is discussed in detail in the following sections.

c. Output Signal   This is the time course of the concentration of any one of the components in the system: namely, S_1, S_2, A, B, P_1, and P_2. Thus, the basic system described can produce six output signals.

4.1.3   Analytical Models for the Basic System

The analytical models developed in this part of the study describe the performance of the basic system and allow one to predict the output signal produced by the system when its operational parameters are known. Unlike previous work [76–86], these models explicitly take into account the operational mode of the system (i.e., the reactor type in which the reactions involved take place). This approach was taken in order not only to use these analytical models for numerical simulations, but also to allow us to interpret the experimental results obtained using real systems (Section 4.3) and to assess the validity of the analytical models employed. The models developed are based on mass balances of the components involved and on the characteristics related to the particular reactor used. Unless otherwise indicated, the simulations described below were carried out using these types of input signals with variations of the parameters defined above.

4.1.3.1   Basic System in a Fed-Batch Reactor Configuration

In the fed-batch (semicontinuous) operation mode, substrates are fed into the reactor but no material is removed from the reactor. Therefore, the total volume of the material within the reactor increases as a function of time. For this reactor type the mass balance for each component of the reaction mixture is given by

$$\frac{d(VC_j)}{dt} = Q_j C_{j,0} + r_j V \tag{3}$$

where C_j = concentration of component j in the reactor
$C_{j,0}$ = concentration of component j in the feed stream
t = time
V = volume of the reaction mixture
Q_j = volumetric flow rate of the inlet stream feeding component j
r_j = rate of production of component j by reaction

Expanding the derivative in equation (3) gives

$$\frac{d(VC_j)}{dt} = V\frac{dC_j}{dt} + C_j\frac{dV}{dt} \tag{4}$$

Assuming that the density of the reaction mixture is not affected by the inlet streams, equation (4) can be simplified:

$$\frac{d(VC_j)}{dt} = V\frac{dC_j}{dt} + C_j\sum Q_j \tag{5}$$

Combining equations (3) and (5), we obtain

$$\frac{dC_j}{dt} = \frac{1}{V}\left(C_{j,0}Q_j - C_j\sum Q_j\right) + r_j \tag{6}$$

We note here that

$$V = V_0 + t\sum Q_j$$

where V_0 is the initial volume of the reaction mixture.

Equation (6) can be used for each component in the basic system, and this leads to equations (7) to (14). In these equations it is assumed that only the substrates S_1 and S_2 enter the reactor in the feed stream, with the concentrations $[S_1]_0$ and $[S_2]_0$. Moreover, the feed stream has a constant flow rate, Q. It should be noted that the concentrations $[S_1]_0$ and $[S_2]_0$ vary with time.

$$\frac{d\,[S_1]}{dt} = \frac{Q}{V_0 + Qt}([S_1]_0 - [S_1]) - r_1 \tag{7}$$

$$\frac{d\,[S_2]}{dt} = \frac{Q}{V_0 + Qt}([S_2]_0 - [S_2]) - r_2 \tag{8}$$

$$\frac{d\,[A]}{dt} = -\frac{Q}{V_0 + Qt}[A] - r_1 + r_2 \tag{9}$$

$$\frac{d\,[B]}{dt} = -\frac{Q}{V_0 + Qt}[B] + r_1 - r_2 \tag{10}$$

$$\frac{d\,[P_1]}{dt} = -\frac{Q}{V_0 + Qt}[P_1] + r_1 \tag{11}$$

$$\frac{d\,[P_2]}{dt} = -\frac{Q}{V_0 + Qt}\,[P_2] + r_2 \tag{12}$$

$$\frac{d\,[E_1]}{dt} = -\frac{Q}{V_0 + Qt}\,[E_1] \tag{13}$$

$$\frac{d\,[E_2]}{dt} = -\frac{Q}{V_0 + Qt}\,[E_2] \tag{14}$$

where r_1 is the rate equation for reaction (1) and r_2 is the rate equation for reaction (2).

Equations (7) to (12) are related to the reaction mechanism considered. In the models developed in this work, several mechanisms were considered and they are detailed in the following subsections. In all these mechanisms the enzyme concentrations are included in the maximum reaction rates, $V_{m,i}$, as defined by

$$V_{m,i} = k_i\,[E_i] \qquad i = 1, 2 \tag{15}$$

where k_i is the rate constant for product production.

Initial conditions for equations (7) to (14) are defined by the concentrations of the substrates, products, and enzymes in the reactor at the onset of operation (at time $t = 0$), according to

$$
\begin{aligned}
&[S_1] = 0, && [S_2] = 0 \\
&[P_1] = 0, && [P_2] = 0 \\
&[A] = [A]_{t=0}, && [B] = 0 \\
&[E_1] = [E_1]_{t=0}, && [E_2] = [E_2]_{t=0}
\end{aligned}
\tag{16}
$$

Equations (7) to (14) are solved numerically according to the Runge–Kutta method [145], with initial conditions as defined in equation (16).

a. Ping-Pong Mechanism   In the basic system two substrates and two products are involved in each reaction. For this case a commonly encountered mechanism is the ping-pong type [146,147], and the reaction sequence for this mechanism is written in equation (17) in terms of reaction (1). In this sequence the first product, P_1, dissociates from the enzyme before the binding of the second substrate, A, and the enzyme oscillates between two stable forms, E and F.

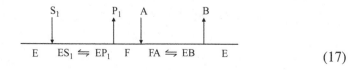

$$\tag{17}$$

For this mechanism type, when both reactions in the basic system are not reversible and inhibition is not involved, the reaction rates r_1 and r_2 are given by equations (18) and (19) [146]:

$$r_1 = \frac{V_{m,1}[S_1][A]}{K_{m,A}[S_1] + K_{m,S_1}[A] + [S_1][A]} \tag{18}$$

$$r_2 = \frac{V_{m,2}[S_2][B]}{K_{m,B}[S_2] + K_{m,S_2}[B] + [S_2][B]} \tag{19}$$

b. Ping-Pong Mechanism and Reversible Reactions In this case, instead of reactions (1) and (2), respectively, we consider reactions 1r and 2r respectively

$$S_1 + A \rightleftharpoons P_1 + B \qquad \text{reaction (1r)} \tag{20}$$

$$S_2 + B \rightleftharpoons P_2 + B \qquad \text{reaction (2r)} \tag{21}$$

When the reaction mechanisms for all the processes are of the ping-pong type, the reaction rates are given by equations (22) and (23) [146]:

$$r_1 = \frac{V_{m,1}[S_1][A]}{K_{m,A}[S_1] + K_{m,S_1}[A] + [S_1][A]} - \frac{V_{m,-1}[P_1][B]}{K_{m,B}[P_1] + K_{m,P_1}[B] + [P_1][B]} \tag{22}$$

$$r_2 = \frac{V_{m,2}[S_2][B]}{K_{m,B}[S_2] + K_{m,S_2}[B] + [S_2][B]} - \frac{V_{m,-2}[P_2][A]}{K_{m,A}[P_2] + K_{m,P_2}[A] + [P_2][A]} \tag{23}$$

c. Ping-Pong Mechanism and Product Inhibition The reactions considered here are described by equations (1) and (2); in addition, products P_1 and P_2 are considered to be competitive inhibitors of enzymes E_1 and E_2, respectively. Under these conditions, assuming that P_1 and P_2 compete with S_1 and S_2, respectively, the following equations hold for r_1 and r_2 [146]:

$$r_1 = \frac{V_{m,1}[S_1][A]}{\left\{1 + K_{b,1}[P_1]/K_{q,1}[A] + [P_1]/K_{q,1}\right\} K_{m,S_1}[A] + K_{m,A}[S_1] + [S_1][A]} \tag{24}$$

$$r_2 = \frac{V_{m,2}[S_2][B]}{\left\{1 + K_{b,2}[P_2]/K_{q,2}[B] + [P_2]/K_{q,2}\right\} K_{m,S_2}[B] + K_{m,B}[S_2] + [S_2][B]} \tag{25}$$

A related case is when products B and A are considered to be inhibitors of enzymes E_1 and E_2, respectively. When B and A compete with A and B, respectively, the following equations hold for r_1 and r_2 [146]:

$$r_1 = \frac{V_{m,1}[S_1][A]}{\left\{1 + K_{b,1}[B]/K_{q,1}[S_1] + [B]/K_{q,1}\right\} K_{m,A}[S_1] + K_{m,S_1}[A] + [S_1][A]}$$

(26)

$$r_2 = \frac{V_{m,2}[S_2][B]}{\left\{1 + K_{b,2}[A]/K_{q,2}[S_2] + [A]/K_{q,2}\right\} K_{m,B}[S_2] + K_{m,S_2}[B] + [S_2][B]}$$

(27)

d. Ordered Bi–Bi Mechanism   For reactions in which two substrates yield two products, an additional mechanism can be considered the ordered bi–bi. In this mechanism, which is described schematically by equation (28) [146,147] in terms of reaction (1), it is impossible for B to bind until after S_1 binds and promotes a conformational change in the enzyme that exposes the B binding site.

$$ (28) $$

For this case, and when both reactions in the basic system are not reversible and inhibition is not involved, the reaction rates r_1 and r_2 become

$$r_1 = \frac{V_{m,2}[S_1][A]}{K_{m,A}[S_1] + K_{m,S_1}[A] + [S_1][A] + K_a K_{m,S_1}}$$

(29)

$$r_2 = \frac{V_{m,1}[S_2][B]}{K_{m,B}[S_2] + K_{m,S_2}[B] + [S_2][B] + K_b K_{m,S_2}}$$

(30)

4.1.3.2   Basic System in Continuous Operation: CSTR and Packed Bed Configuration Reactors

For the convenience of numerical solution, the continuous reactor is modeled in terms of compartmental analysis, as shown schematically in Figure 4.3. The reactor is modeled as a series of *n* compartments, each one a homogeneous CSTR [148]. The compartments are all assumed to have the same volume. Applying the compartmental analysis approach enables consideration

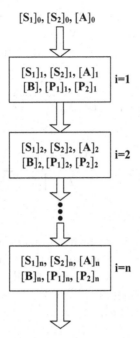

Figure 4.3 Compartmental modeling of the reactor. The index i indicates the compartment number.

of backmixing effects, which can be quantified by the parameter n (number of compartments). Thus, for extensive backmixing, the reactor approaches the behavior of a CSTR, and in this case, $n = 1$. On the other hand, when backmixing effects are not operative at all, the reactor behaves as a plug flow reactor (PFR) and is theoretically characterized by $n = \infty$. Actually, when $n = 5$ the reactor can be defined as a PFR [148]. When $1 < n < 5$, the reactor is defined here as a packed bed reactor.

For the reactor described in Figure 4.3, the general mass balance for component j at stage i is

$$\frac{dC_{j,i}}{dt} = \frac{Q}{V_i}\left(C_{j,i-1} - C_{j,i}\right) + r_{j,i} \tag{31}$$

where $C_{j,i}$ = concentration of component j in the ith compartment
        t = time
        V_i = volume of the ith compartment
        Q = volumetric flow rate through the reactor
        $r_{j,i}$ = rate of production of component j by reaction, in the ith compartment

Equation (31) was written using the following assumptions:

- Each compartment is a homogeneous CSTR.
- The immobilized enzymes are distributed homogeneously in the reactor.
- No diffusion limitations (internal or external) are operative in the reactor.

Equation (31) can be applied for each of the components in the basic system, and this leads to the equations

$$\frac{d\,[S_1]_i}{dt} = \frac{Q}{V_i}\left([S_1]_{i-1} - [S_1]_i\right) - r_{1,i} \tag{32}$$

$$\frac{d\,[S_2]_i}{dt} = \frac{Q}{V_i}\left([S_2]_{i-1} - [S_2]_i\right) - r_{2,i} \tag{33}$$

$$\frac{d\,[A]_i}{dt} = \frac{Q}{V_i}\left([A]_{i-1} - [A]_i\right) - r_{1,i} + r_{2,i} \tag{34}$$

$$\frac{d\,[B]_i}{dt} = \frac{Q}{V_i}\left([B]_{i-1} - [B]_i\right) + r_{1,i} - r_{2,i} \tag{35}$$

$$\frac{d\,[P_1]_i}{dt} = \frac{Q}{V_i}\left([P_1]_{i-1} - [P_1]_i\right) + r_{1,i} \tag{36}$$

$$\frac{d\,[P_2]_i}{dt} = \frac{Q}{V_i}\left([P_2]_{i-1} - [P_2]_i\right) + r_{2,i} \tag{37}$$

where $r_{1,i}$ is the rate equation for reaction (1) in the ith compartment and $r_{2,i}$ is the rate equation for reaction (2) in the ith compartment.

Equations (32) to (37) are related to the reaction mechanism considered. In the models developed in this work, several mechanisms were considered, and they are detailed in the following subsections. Initial conditions for equations (32) to (37) are defined by the concentrations of the substrates, products, and enzymes in the reactor compartments at the onset of operation (at time $t = 0$), for $1 \leq i \leq n$, according to

$$\begin{array}{ll}
[S_1]_i = 0, & [S_2]_i = 0 \\
[P_1]_i = 0, & [P_2]_i = 0 \\
[A]_i = 0, & [B]_i = 0
\end{array} \tag{38}$$

As indicated in Figure 4.4, the feed stream to the reactor is composed of the substrates S_1 and S_2 and the cofactor A. Thus, for any time t equation (39) holds:

$$\begin{array}{ll}
[S_1]_0 = f_1\,(t), & [S_2]_0 = f_2\,(t) \\
[P_1]_0 = 0, & [P_2]_0 = 0 \\
[A]_0 = f_3\,(t), & [B]_0 = 0
\end{array} \tag{39}$$

hold. Equations (32) to (37) are solved numerically according to the Runge–Kutta method [145], with the initial conditions defined in equation (38).

a. Ping-Pong Mechanism   When the ping-pong mechanism [146,147] described in equation (17) is considered, the following equations are used for $r_{1,i}$ and $r_{2,i}$, respectively:

$$r_{1,i} = \frac{V_{m,1}[S_1]_i[A]_i}{K_{m,A}[S_1]_i + K_{m,S_1}[A]_i + [S_1]_i[A]_i} \tag{40}$$

$$r_{2,i} = \frac{V_{m,2}[S_2]_i[B]_i}{K_{m,B}[S_2]_i + K_{m,S_2}[B]_i + [S_2]_i[B]_i} \tag{41}$$

These equations are similar to equations (18) and (19) but include indices for the compartment number.

b. Ping-Pong Mechanism and Reversible Reactions   When the reactions in the basic system are reversible and follow the ping-pong mechanism, as indicated in equations (20) and (21), the following equations are used for $r_{1,i}$ and $r_{2,i}$ respectively:

$$r_{1,i} = \frac{V_{m,1}[S_1]_i[A]_i}{K_{m,A}[S_1]_i + K_{m,S_1}[A]_i + [S_1]_i[A]_i} - \frac{V_{m,-1}[P_1]_i[B]_i}{K_{m,B}[P_1]_i + K_{m,P_1}[B]_i + [P_1]_i[B]_i} \tag{42}$$

$$r_{2,i} = \frac{V_{m,2}[S_2]_i[B]_i}{K_{m,B}[S_2]_i + K_{m,S_2}[B]_i + S_2[B]_i} - \frac{V_{m,-2}[P_2]_i[A]_i}{K_{m,A}[P_2]_i + K_{m,P_2}[A]_i + [P_2]_i[A]_i} \tag{43}$$

These equations are similar to equations (22) and (23) but include indices for the compartment number.

c. Ping-Pong Mechanism and Product Inhibition   When product B or A is inhibitory to enzyme E_1 or E_2, respectively, assuming that B competes with A in reaction (1) and that A competes with B in reaction (2), the reaction rates considered are [146]

$$r_{1,i} = \frac{V_{m,1}[S_1]_i[A]_i}{\{1 + [B]_i/K_{i,B}\}\,K_{m,A_1}[S_1]_i + K_{m,S_1}[A]_i + [S_1]_i[A]_i} \tag{44}$$

$$r_{2,i} = \frac{V_{m,2}[S_2]_i[B]_i}{\{1 + [A]_i/K_{i,A}\}\,K_{m,B}[S_1]_i + K_{m,S_2}[B]_i + [S_2]_i[B]_i} \tag{45}$$

d. Ping-Pong Mechanism and Internal Inhibition   The case when one of the substrates of reaction (1), namely S_1, is inhibitory to enzyme E_2 was also considered. In the commonly used nomenclature, substrate 1 is an external inhibitor in the process promoted by enzyme E_2. However, S_1 is part of the system considered in this study (i.e., the basic system shown in Figure 4.1). Therefore, we here introduce the ad hoc nomenclature *internal inhibitor* to indicate a compound that is part of the system considered and at the same time acts as an inhibitor in the reaction in which it is not involved directly. In this case, the rate equation for reaction (2) when the inhibitor S_1 competes with S_2 becomes

$$r_{2,i} = \frac{V_{m,2}[S_2]_i[B]_i}{\left\{1 + [S_1]_i/K_{i,S_1}\right\} K_{m,S_2}[B]_i + K_{m,B}[S_2]_i + [S_2]_i[B]_i} \tag{46}$$

e. Ordered Bi–Bi Mechanism   When the ordered bi–bi type [146,147] described by equation (28) was considered, and for the case when both reactions in the basic system are not reversible and inhibition is not involved, the following equations are used for $r_{1,i}$ and $r_{2,i}$, respectively:

$$r_{1,i} = \frac{V_{m,2}[S_1]_i[A]_i}{K_{m,A}[S_1]_i + K_{m,S_1}[A]_i + [S_1]_i[A]_i + K_a K_{m,S_1}} \tag{47}$$

$$r_{2,i} = \frac{V_{m,1}[S_2]_i[B]_i}{K_{m,B}[S_2]_i + K_{m,S_2}[B]_i + [S_2]_i[B]_i + K_b K_{m,S_2}} \tag{48}$$

These equations are similar to equations (29) and (30) but include indices for the compartment number.

4.1.4 Results of Numerical Simulations for the Basic System

The basic system was designed to operate as an information-processing unit. As such, the output signal should differ from the input signal in at least one property: type, cycle time, or amplitude. As part of this research, many numerical simulations have been carried out. The results presented here are only a fraction of what was done. They were chosen as being representative of the abilities of the systems considered to perform information-processing tasks, and also to reveal the main parameters that affect the system achievements.

4.1.4.1 Simulations for a Fed-Batch Reactor

Extensive numerical simulations were performed for the basic system when operated as a fed-batch reactor. The sets of basic values used for the parameters

Table 4.1 Numerical Values of the Operational Parameters Used in Simulations of Fed-Batch and Continuous Reactors

Parameter	Symbol	Units	Set I	Set II
Initial volume of the reaction mixture	V_0	mL	5	50
Volume of the continuous reactor	V	mL	5	50
Volumetric flow rate	Q	mL/h	0.6	8
Cycle time	τ	min	20	5
Concentration range of S_1 in the feed stream	$[S_1]_0$	mM	8–12	11–80
Concentration range of S_2 in the feed stream	$[S_2]_0$	mM	8–12	11–80
Initial concentration of A (in a fed-batch reactor)	$[A]_{t=0}$	mM	0.03	0.03
Concentration of A in the feed stream (in a continuous reactor)	$[A]_0$	mM	0.03	0.03
Michaelis constant for S_1	K_{m,S_1}	mM	0.01	0.036
Michaelis constant for S_2	K_{m,S_2}	mM	0.01	0.061
Michaelis constant for A	$K_{m,A}$	mM	0.001	0.0074
Michaelis constant for B	$K_{m,B}$	mM	0.001	0.0076
Maximal rate of reaction (1) $S_1 + A \rightarrow P_1 + B$	$V_{m,1}$	mM/min	0.2	0.4
Maximal rate of reaction (2) $S_2 + B \rightarrow P_2 + A$	$V_{m,2}$	mM/min	0.2	0.4

involved are given in Table 4.1. These values are related to a large extent to the experimental systems considered in this study. The results obtained are collected in Figures 4.4 to 4.13 and are presented in the sections below. Table 4.2 summarizes the various system characteristics considered in each figure as well as the operational parameters whose effects were accounted for.

Table 4.2 System Characteristics for Figures 4.4 through 4.13

Figure No.	System Characteristics			
	Mechanism	Reversible Reactions	Inhibition by Product	Effect of:
4.4	Ping-pong	—	—	Time
4.5	Ping-pong	—	—	$V_{m,1}, V_{m,2}$ ($V_{m,1} = V_{m,2}$) on $[S_1]$
4.6	Ping-pong	—	—	$V_{m,1}, V_{m,2}$ ($V_{m,1} = V_{m,2}$) on $[B]$
4.7	Ping-pong	—	—	$V_{m,1}/V_{m,2}$ on $[S_1]$ and $[B]$
4.8	Ping-pong	—	—	$K_{m,j}$ on $[S_1]$ and $[B]$
4.9	Ping-pong	—	—	$[S_1]_0, [S_2]_0$ on $[S_1]$ and $[A]$
4.10	Ping-pong	+	—	K_{eq} on $[B]$
4.11	Ping-pong	—	By A and B	Inhibition by product on $[B]$
4.12	Ping-pong	—	By P_1 and P_2	Inhibition by product on $[B]$
4.13	Ping-pong Ordered Bi–Bi	—	—	Reaction mechanism on $[S_1]$ and $[B]$

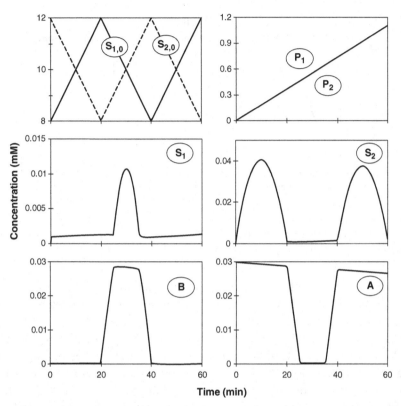

Figure 4.4   Time courses of concentrations of all the reactants in the basic system when operated as a fed-batch reactor. The values of all parameters used are given in Table 4.1, set I.

a. Ping-Pong Mechanism   In Figure 4.4 the time courses of the concentrations of all the reactants in the basic system are presented. The concentrations of S_1 and S_2 in the feed stream, $S_{1,0}$ and $S_{2,0}$, change with time, as shown in the top left panel. These are considered as the input signals. Examination of the concentration profiles obtained for the compounds S_1, S_2, A, B, P_1, and P_2 shows that all these profiles can be considered as output signals containing processed information. It can be seen that in this reactor configuration, products P_1 and P_2 accumulate in the reactor and their concentration profiles are not very useful with respect to information processing, and the discussion about them is limited. The concentration profiles of the substrates, S_1 and S_2, and of the cofactors, A and B, show an interesting behavior, a repetitive signal, completely different from the input signal. In the concentration profiles of A and B, periods of "on" (constant nonzero concentration) and "off" (zero concentration) can be detected; thus, switching characteristics can be observed. In Figures 4.5 to 4.9 the dependence of the output signal characteristics on the system parameters is investigated.

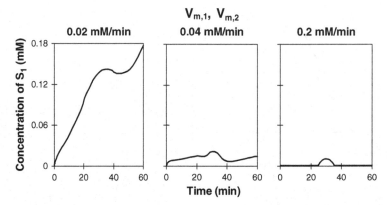

Figure 4.5   Effect of $V_{m,1}$ and $V_{m,2}$ (when $V_{m,1} = V_{m,2}$) on the concentration of S_1 in the basic system when operated as a fed-batch reactor. The values of $V_{m,1}$ and $V_{m,2}$ are indicated above. The values used for all other parameters are given in Table 4.1, set I.

In Figure 4.5 the effect of the maximum reaction rates, $V_{m,1}$ and $V_{m,2}$, on the concentration of S_1 is shown. In these simulations the values of $V_{m,1}$ and $V_{m,2}$ were equal, and $V_{m,i}$ refers to both values ($i = 1$ and 2). The "peak-type" signal obtained with $V_{m,i} = 0.2$ mM cannot be observed with smaller values of $V_{m,i}$ (0.02 and 0.04 mM). In addition, the smaller values of $V_{m,i}$ lead to higher concentrations of S_1 in the reactor due to a low reaction rate and low conversion of S_1. The effect of these rates on the concentration of B is shown in Figure 4.6. It can be seen that the concentration of B is also affected by the values of $V_{m,i}$. Peak-type signals, characterized by a sharp raise and an equally sharp decay, are obtained for the highest value of $V_{m,i}$, and these characteristics disappear for lower values of $V_{m,i}$.

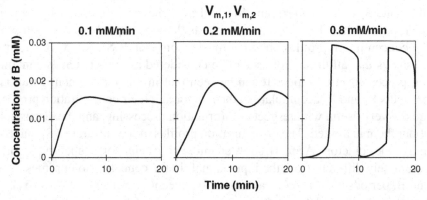

Figure 4.6   Effect of $V_{m,1}$ and $V_{m,2}$ (when $V_{m,1} = V_{m,2}$) on the concentration of B in the basic system when operated as a fed-batch reactor. The values of $V_{m,1}$ and $V_{m,2}$ are indicated above. The values used for all other parameters are given in Table 4.1, set II.

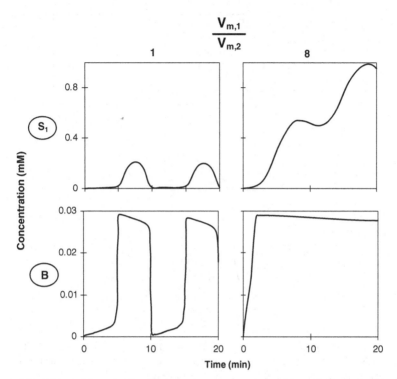

Figure 4.7   Effect of the ratio $V_{m,1}/V_{m,2}$ on the concentrations of S_1 and B in the basic system when operated as a fed-batch reactor. In the left panel $V_{m,1} = V_{m,2} = 0.8$ mM/min and data are taken from Figure 4.6. In the right panel $V_{m,1} = 0.8$ mM/min and $V_{m,2} = 0.1$ mM/min. The values used for all other parameters are given in Table 4.1, set II.

Figure 4.7 shows the effect of the ratio of $V_{m,1}$ to $V_{m,2}$ on the concentrations of S_1 and B. While comparing the cases presented, one can see that when $V_{m,1} > V_{m,2}$, the concentration of S_1 is higher than it is when $V_{m,1} = V_{m,2}$, and the sharp and repetitive characteristics of the signal disappear. Moreover, the concentration profile of B changes from on/off behavior when $V_{m,1} = V_{m,2}$ to almost constant concentration when $V_{m,1} > V_{m,2}$.

Figure 4.8 shows the effect of Michaelis constants on the concentrations of S_1 and B. The results obtained are very similar to those described in Figure 4.7. When $K_{m,j}$ values are multiplied by 10, the concentration of S_1 is higher and the sharp repetitive signal disappears. In addition, the concentration profile of B changes from on/off behavior to almost constant concentration.

Figure 4.9 shows the effect of the range of variation of $S_{1,0}$ and $S_{2,0}$ on the concentrations of S_1 and A. The range is defined as the highest and lowest values of both $S_{1,0}$ and $S_{2,0}$, and their concentrations in the feed stream vary between these values. Decreasing this range causes the disappearance of the sharp signals, as described above.

Michaelis Constansts, $K_{m,j}$ (mM)		
K_{m,S_1}	0.0360	0.360
K_{m,S_2}	0.0610	0.610
$K_{m,A}$	0.0074	0.074
$K_{m,B}$	0.0076	0.076

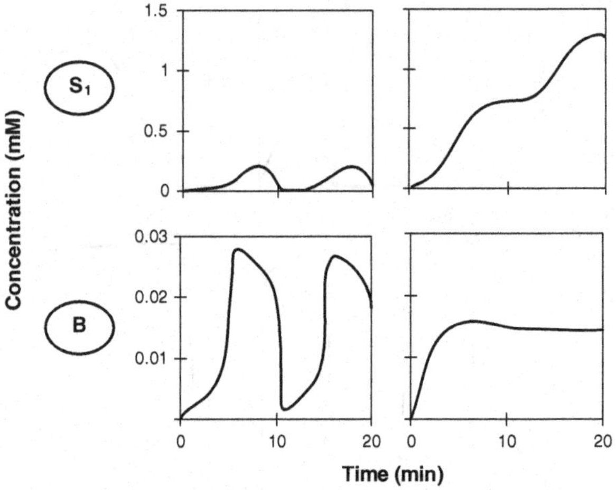

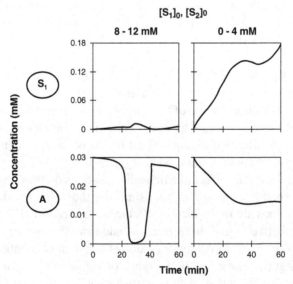

Figure 4.8   Effect of $K_{m,j}$ on the concentrations of S_1 and B in the basic system when operated as a fed-batch reactor. The values of $K_{m,j}$ are indicated on top of each section. The values used for all other parameters are given in Table 4.1, set II.

Figure 4.9   Effect of $[S_1]_0$ and $[S_2]_0$ on the concentrations of S_1 and A in the basic system when operated as a fed-batch reactor. The values of $S_{1,0}$ and $S_{2,0}$ vary between the values indicated on top of each section. The values used for all other parameters are given in Table 4.1, set I.

The simulation results presented here show that the output signals of the system depend to a large extent on the values of $V_{m,i}$, $K_{m,j}$, and $S_{i,0}$ ($i = 1, 2$) and the relationships between them. From the simulations that were carried out in this study, some empirical rules can be derived. Thus, it can be concluded that to get the type of signals described in Figure 4.4, the values of $V_{m,i}$ should be around 20 times the largest value of $K_{m,j}$, and the average values of $S_{i,0}$ should be about 10^3 times the largest value of $K_{m,j}$.

b. Ping-Pong Mechanism and Reversible Reactions   The results shown in Figure 4.10 are representative for the case when both reactions in the basic system are reversible, and also when both directions follow the ping-pong mechanism. This figure presents the effect of K_{eq} on the concentration of B when K_{eq} is defined as the ratio between the maximal reaction rate in the reverse direction ($V_{m,-1}$, $V_{m,-2}$) and the maximal reaction rate in the forward direction ($V_{m,1}$, $V_{m,2}$), respectively; that is, $K_{eq} = V_{m,-1}/V_{m,1} = V_{m,-2}/V_{m,2}$. It can be seen that the increase in K_{eq} from 0 (no reverse reaction) to 0.5 leads to more gradual changes in the concentration of B. However, the on/off behavior observed when $K_{eq} = 0$ and 0.5 disappears when $K_{eq} = 1$, and in the latter case, the concentration of B reaches a constant value.

c. Ping-Pong Mechanism and Product Inhibition   Figures 4.11 and 4.12 show the effect of product inhibition on the concentration of B. In each case considered, one of the products is inhibitory for the enzyme and acts competitively to one of the substrates, as detailed below. The inhibition process is defined by the constants $K_{b,i}$ and $K_{q,i}$. Moreover, inhibition increases

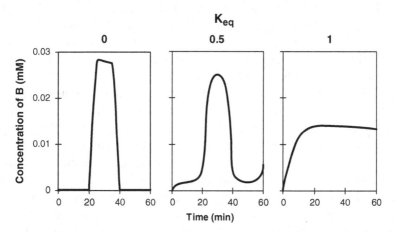

Figure 4.10 Effect of K_{eq} on the concentration of B in the basic system when operated as a fed-batch reactor. The values of K_{eq} are indicated above. The values used for all other parameters are given in Table 4.1, set I.

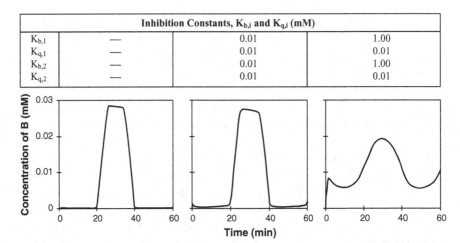

Inhibition Constants, $K_{b,i}$ and $K_{q,i}$ (mM)			
$K_{b,1}$	—	0.01	1.00
$K_{q,1}$	—	0.01	0.01
$K_{b,2}$	—	0.01	1.00
$K_{q,2}$	—	0.01	0.01

Figure 4.11 Effect of inhibition of enzyme 2 by cofactor A and of enzyme 1 by cofactor B (i.e., product inhibition) on the concentration of B in the basic system when operated as a fed-batch reactor. For the central and right panels the inhibition constants are indicated on top of each section. In the left panel, inhibition by products was not considered, and—indicates that the parameter is not applicable. Data presented in the left panel are taken from Figure 4.4. The values used for all other parameters ares given in Table 4.1, set I.

when increasing the value of $K_{b,i}$ and/or with decreasing the value $K_{q,i}$. In Figure 4.11, B is considered as the inhibitor in reaction (1) (i.e., $S_1 + A \rightarrow P_1 + B$) that competes with the cofactor A, and A is considered as the inhibitor in reaction (2) (i.e., $S_2 + B \rightarrow P_2 + A$) that competes with the cofactor B. Comparison of the results obtained for the case when product inhibition does not take place (left panel) to those obtained when product inhibition is operative (central and right panels) indicates that for small values of $K_{b,i}$ the concentration profile of B is not affected significantly (central panel). However, increasing the values of $K_{b,i}$ causes enhanced changes in the concentration profile of B (right panel).

In Figure 4.12, P_1 is considered as the inhibitor in reaction (1) (i.e., $S_1 + A \rightarrow P_1 + B$) that competes with substrate S_1, and P_2 is considered as the inhibitor in reaction (2) (i.e., $S_2 + B \rightarrow P_2 + A$) that competes with substrate S_2. In this case the effects of product inhibition on the concentration profile of B are significant even when considering low values of $K_{b,i}$ (central panel). This is probably due to the fact that P_1 and P_2 accumulate in the reactor and reach higher concentrations than B and A in the case presented in Figure 4.11. In the case shown here, when product inhibition is operative, the on/off behavior (left panel) dissapears and a decaying output signal is obtained (central panel). This decay of the output signal's amplitude is motivated by the accumulation of the inhibitors in the reactor during the

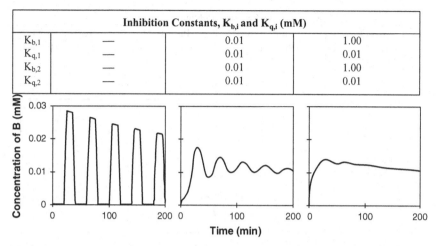

Inhibition Constants, $K_{b,i}$ and $K_{q,i}$ (mM)			
$K_{b,1}$	—	0.01	1.00
$K_{q,1}$	—	0.01	0.01
$K_{b,2}$	—	0.01	1.00
$K_{q,2}$	—	0.01	0.01

Figure 4.12 Effect of inhibition of enzyme 1 by product P_1 and of enzyme 2 by product P_2 on the concentration of B in the basic system when operated as a fed-batch reactor. For the central and right panels the inhibition constants are indicated on top of each section. In the left panel, inhibition by products was not considered, and—indicates that the parameter is not applicable. Data presented in the left panel are taken from Figure 4.8. The values used for all other parameters ares given in Table 4.1, set I.

process, and this effect is enhaced when the values of $K_{b,i}$ are increased from 0.01 to 1.00 (right panel).

d. Reactions with Different Mechanisms   Figure 4.13 presents the effect of reaction mechanisms on the concentrations of S_1 and B. In the simulations above, all the reactions are assumed to be of the ping-pong type, and this case is presented for comparison in the left panel. In the central panel one reaction is assumed to be of the ping-pong type, and the other is assumed to be of the ordered bi–bi type. In the right panel both reactions are assumed to be of the ordered bi–bi type. It can be seen that different reaction mechanisms induce different concentration profiles. Thus, the reaction mechanism should be an important factor in the design of these systems.

4.1.4.2 Simulations for Continuous-Operation Reactors

In Section 4.1.4.1 results of numerical simulations were presented for the case when the basic system is operated as a fed-batch reactor. In this section, results of the numerical simulations are presented for the case when the basic system is operated in continuous reactors. The results were obtained for several reactor types. In terms of compartmental analysis (see Section 4.1.3.2) these types are determined by the number of compartments (n) considered to make up the reactor (see Figure 4.3). Three cases are presented here: $n = 1$

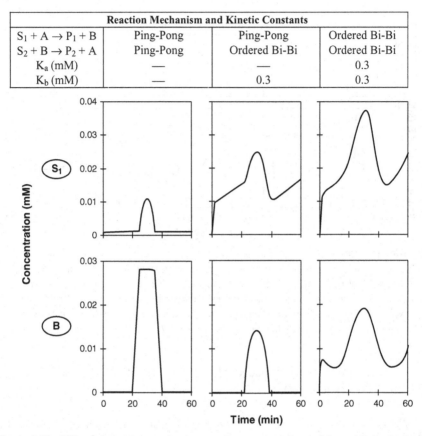

Reaction Mechanism and Kinetic Constants			
$S_1 + A \rightarrow P_1 + B$	Ping-Pong	Ping-Pong	Ordered Bi-Bi
$S_2 + B \rightarrow P_2 + A$	Ping-Pong	Ordered Bi-Bi	Ordered Bi-Bi
K_a (mM)	—	—	0.3
K_b (mM)	—	0.3	0.3

Figure 4.13 Effect of reaction mechanism on the concentrations of S_1 and B in the basic system when operated as a fed-batch reactor. The kinetic mechanism and the values of the parameters K_a and K_b are indicated on top of each section;—indicates that the parameter is not applicable for the ping-pong mechanism. The values used for all other parameters are given in Table 4.1, set I.

for a CSTR, $n = 3$ for a packed bed reactor with backmixing, and $n = 5$ for a PFR.

a. Ping-Pong Kinetics   Figures 4.14 to 4.27 present the concentrations of the basic system components at the reactor outlet when the only processes involved are the ones indicated in reactions (1) and (2). The simulations were carried out for different reactor types and with different values of flow rate (Q), concentration of cofactor A in the feed ([A]$_0$), maximum reaction rates ($V_{m,i}$) and the cycle time of the input signal (τ). The sets of the basic values used for the parameters involved are given in Table 4.1.

In the case presented in Figure 4.14, a CSTR is considered, and it can be seen that two types of useful output signals are obtained. One is represented

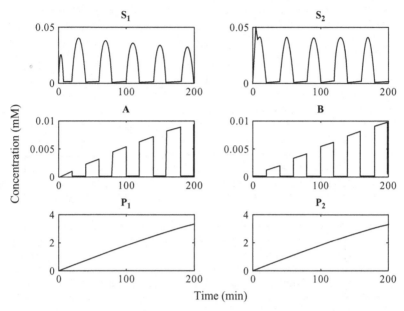

Figure 4.14 Performance of the basic system when operated as a CSTR ($n = 1$). Concentrations of all the reactants are indicated for the reactor outlet. The values of all parameters used are given in Table 4.1, set I.

by the concentration profiles of S_1 and S_2, and the second is represented by the concentration profiles of the cofactors A and B. However, in both cases, periods of "on" and "off" that last 20 min are observed. Thus, the system acts as a switching machine with periods of 20 min.

The system considered in Figure 4.15 differs from the one in Figure 4.14 in the number of compartments considered in the reactor (n). It can be seen that when three compartments are considered, different information processing takes place, and regarding the concentration profiles of S_1 and B the system acts as a rectifier. Very similar behavior is obtained when n is considered to be 5, and the reactor is actually a PFR. These results are presented in Figure 4.16. In this case the system acts as a rectifier regarding the concentration profiles of S_1, S_2, and B.

The results represented in Figure 4.17 are obtained when the system is operated as a CSTR with $Q = 6$ mL/h. It can be seen that after the transient time, oscillatory output signals with a period time of 40 min are obtained and they are represented by the concentration profiles of S_1, S_2, A, and B. Thus, this system converts the sharp input signals to oscillatory signals with the same period of time of the input signal (40 min) but with different amplitudes. Very similar behavior is observed when a PFR is considered ($n = 5$), and these results are presented in Figure 4.18.

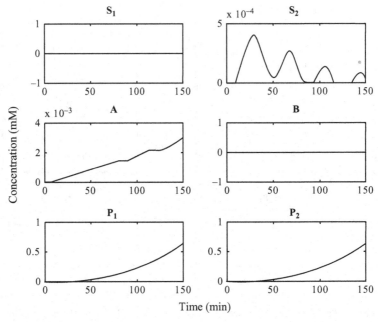

Figure 4.15   Performance of the basic system when operated as a packed bed reactor ($n = 3$). Concentrations of all the reactants are indicated for the reactor outlet. The values of all parameters used are given in Table 4.1, set I.

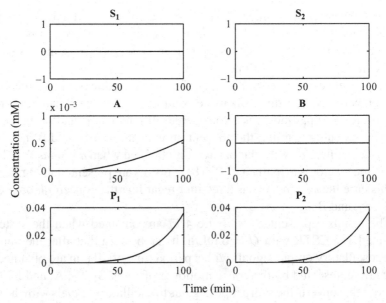

Figure 4.16   Performance of the basic system when operated as a PFR ($n = 5$). Concentrations of all the reactants are indicated for the reactor outlet. The values of all parameters used are given in Table 4.1, set I.

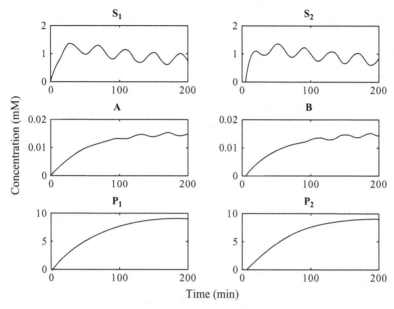

Figure 4.17 Performance of the basic system when operated as a CSTR ($n = 1$). Concentrations of all the reactants are indicated for the reactor outlet. Calculations were performed with $Q = 6$ mL/h. The values used for all other parameters are given in Table 4.1, set I.

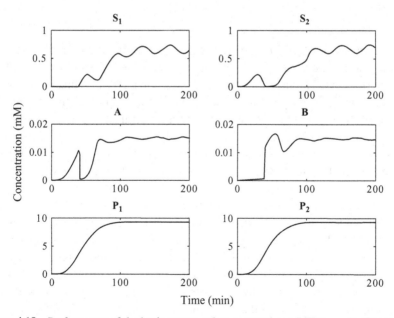

Figure 4.18 Performance of the basic system when operated as a PFR ($n = 5$). Concentrations of all the reactants are indicated for the reactor outlet. Calculations were performed with $Q = 6$ mL/h. The values used for all other parameters are given in Table 4.1, set I.

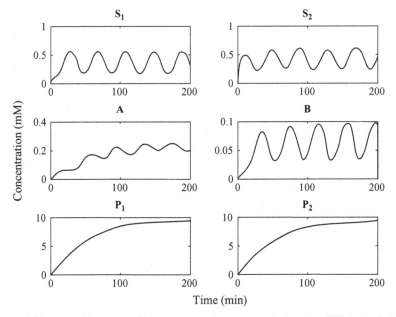

Figure 4.19 Performance of the basic system when operated as a CSTR ($n = 1$). Concentrations of all the reactants are indicated for the reactor outlet. Calculations were performed with $Q = 6$ mL/h and $[A]_0 = 0.3$ mM. The values used for all other parameters are given in Table 4.1, set I.

In Figures 4.19, 4.20, and 4.21 three operation modes are considered: CSTR, packed bed, and PFR, respectively. In these figures $Q = 6$ mL/h and $[A]_0 = 0.3$ mM. The information processing carried out by this system is also conversion of the sharp input signals to oscillatory signals with the same time period of the input signal but with different amplitudes. Moreover, unlike the case presented in Figure 4.17, in which all the signals were synchronized, phase shifts here are observed between the output signals. However, the cases when $n = 3$ (Figure 4.20) and $n = 5$ (Figure 4.21) are very similar to one another.

In Figures 4.22 and 4.23 simulations were also carried out with $Q = 6$ mL/h, $[A]_0 = 0.3$ mM but with $V_{m,i} = 0.1$ mM/min and considering a CSTR and a PFR, respectively. The output signal represented by the concentration profiles of S_1 and S_2 when a CSTR is employed (Figure 4.22) is an oscillatory signal resembling those obtained in Figures 4.19 to 4.21. However, the concentration profiles of A and B reach constant concentrations after the transient time. This is also the case when a PFR is employed in Figure 4.23.

Figure 4.24 presents results obtained for a CSTR with $Q = 6$ mL/h, $[A]_0 = 0.3$ mM, and $V_{m,i} = 0.4$ mM/min. In this case four different types of output signal are observed, and these are presented by the concentration

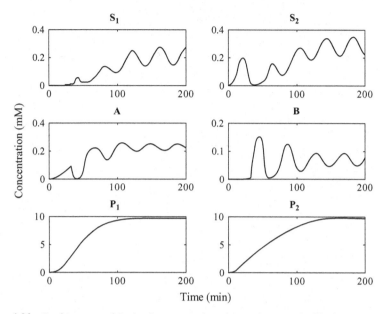

Figure 4.20 Performance of the basic system when operated as a packed bed reactor ($n = 3$). Concentrations of all the reactants are indicated for the reactor outlet. Calculations were performed with $Q = 6$ mL/h and $[A]_0 = 0.3$ mM. The values used for all other parameters are given in Table 4.1, set I.

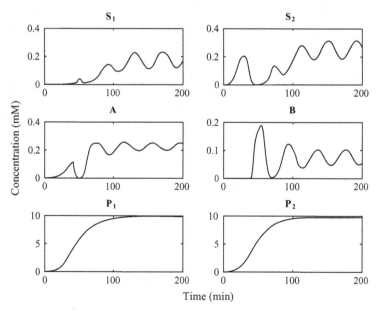

Figure 4.21 Performance of the basic system when operated as a PFR ($n = 5$). Concentrations of all the reactants are indicated for the reactor outlet. Calculations were performed with $Q = 6$ mL/h and $[A]_0 = 0.3$ mM. The values used for all other parameters are given in Table 4.1, set I.

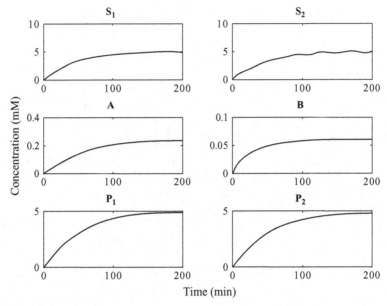

Figure 4.22 Performance of the basic system when operated as a CSTR ($n = 1$). Concentrations of all the reactants are indicated for the reactor outlet. Calculations were performed with $Q = 6$ mL/h, $[A]_0 = 0.3$ mM and $V_{m,i} = 0.1$ mM/min. The values used for all other parameters are given in Table 4.1, set I.

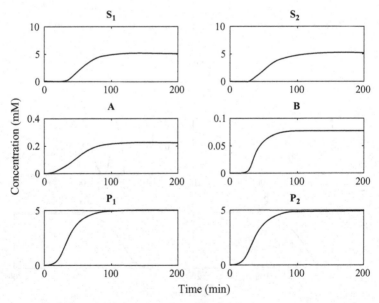

Figure 4.23 Performance of the basic system when operated as a PFR ($n = 5$). Concentrations of all the reactants are indicated for the reactor outlet. Calculations were performed with $Q = 6$ mL/h, $[A]_0 = 0.3$ mM, and $V_{m,i} = 0.1$ mM/min. The values used for all other parameters are given in Table 4.1, set I.

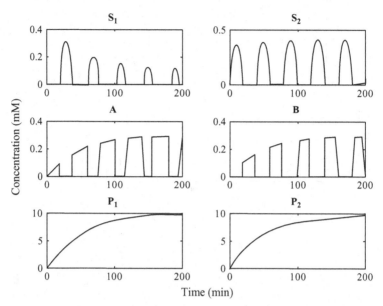

Figure 4.24 Performance of the basic system when operated as a CSTR ($n = 1$). Concentrations of all the reactants are indicated for the reactor outlet. Calculations were performed with $Q = 6$ mL/h, $[A]_0 = 0.3$ mM, and $V_{m,i} = 0.4$ mM/min. The values used for all other parameters are given in Table 4.1, set I.

profiles of S_1, S_2, A, and B. It can be seen that the concentration profile of S_1 is a bell type of signal that appears every 30 min and lasts 10 min. Similar characteristics but with different parameters are observed in the concentration profile of S_2. Here the signal appears every 20 min and lasts 20 min. In addition, the concentration profiles of A and B also show "on" and "off" periods, when for A the "on" period is 30 min and the "off" period is 10 min, and for B both "on" and "off" periods last 20 min.

The results obtained with the same parameters employed in Figure 4.24 but considering a PFR rather than a CSTR are shown in Figure 4.25. In this case, regarding the concentration profile of S_1, after one sharp peak the system acts as a rectifier. The concentration profiles of S_2 and B are characterized by bell-shaped signals that appear every 20 min, and they appear with a phase shift of 20 min. The signal represented by the concentration profile of A is a repetitive signal with a time period of 40 min.

Figure 4.26 presents the results obtained for a CSTR with $Q = 6$ mL/h, $[A]_0 = 0.3$ mM, and a cycle time of 5 min. In this case the time period of the output signals represented by S_1, S_2, and B is reduced to 10 min. Results for the case when a PFR is employed with the same parameter values are presented in Figure 4.27. Here the oscillations disappear and all the concentration profiles reach a constant value after the transient time.

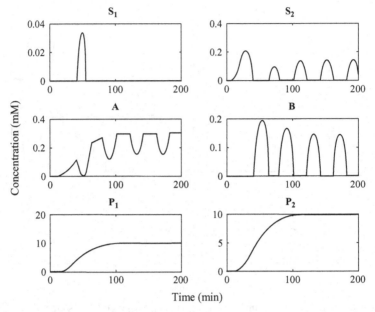

Figure 4.25 Performance of the basic system when operated as a PFR ($n = 5$). Concentrations of all the reactants are indicated for the reactor outlet. Calculations were performed with $Q = 6$ mL/h, $[A]_0 = 0.3$ mM, and $V_{m,i} = 0.4$ mM/min. The values used for all other parameters are given in Table 4.1, set I.

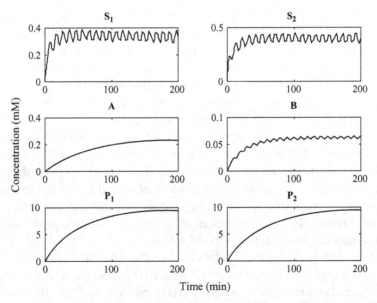

Figure 4.26 Performance of the basic system when operated as a CSTR ($n = 1$). Concentrations of all the reactants are indicated for the reactor outlet. Calculations were performed with $Q = 6$ mL/h, $[A]_0 = 0.3$ mM, and a cycle time (τ) of 5 min. The values used for all other parameters are given in Table 4.1, set I.

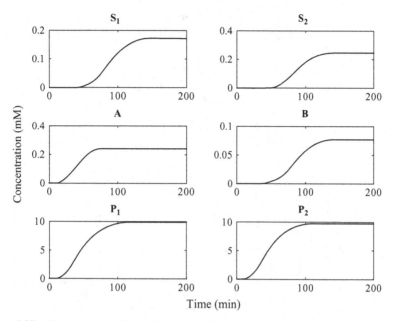

Figure 4.27 Performance of the basic system when operated as a PFR ($n = 5$). Concentrations of all the reactants are indicated for the reactor outlet. Calculations were performed with $Q = 6$ mL/h, $[A]_0 = 0.3$ mM, and a cycle time (τ) of 5 min. The values used for all other parameters are given in Table 4.1, set I.

From Figures 4.14 to 4.27 it can be seen that the concentration profiles of products P_1 and P_2 are not remarkably different in the various cases presented, and in most cases a constant steady-state concentration is reached for them. Therefore, the useful signals as a means of information processing are obtained with the concentration profiles of S_1, S_2, A, and B.

To examine the effects of the parameters involved on the reactor performance (i.e., on the output signals obtained), the results of the numerical simulations presented in Figures 4.14 to 4.27 were replotted in Figures 4.28 to 4.35. The effect of the reactor type on the concentration profiles of S_1 and B is shown in Figure 4.28. The results were obtained for three reactor types, all operated under the same set of parameters. It can be seen that the concentration profiles presented are affected by the reactor type considered. The signals obtained with the fed-batch reactor and the CSTR are of the same type but with different concentration ranges. However, a different situation is encountered for the PFR. In this case neither S_1 nor B is present in the reactor outlet, as they are consumed completely due to a very high residence time in the reactor (500 min) and to the fact that no backmixing is involved.

Figure 4.29 shows the effect of the flow rate on the concentrations of S_1 and A when the CSTR is considered. When the flow rate is increased from

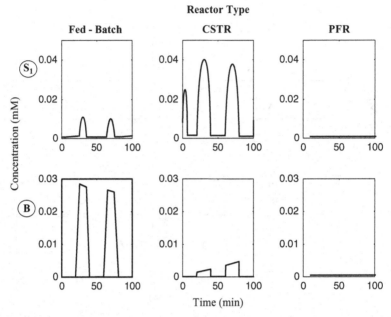

Figure 4.28 Effect of reactor type on the concentrations of S_1 and A in the basic system. The reactor types are indicated at the top of each section. Data for fed-batch, CSTR, and PFR are taken from Figures 4.4, 4.14, and 4.16, respectively.

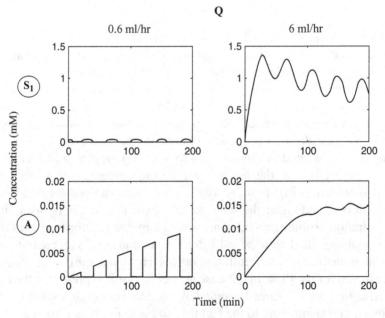

Figure 4.29 Effect of flow rate on the concentrations of S_1 and A in the basic system when operated as a CSTR ($n = 1$). The values of Q are indicated at the top of each section. Data for $Q = 0.6$ mL/h and $Q = 6$ mL/h are taken from Figures 4.14 and 4.17, respectively.

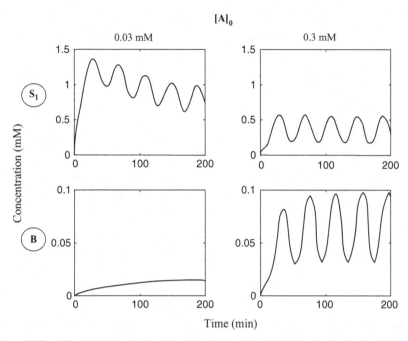

Figure 4.30 Effect of $[A]_0$ on the concentrations of S_1 and B in the basic system when operated as a CSTR ($n = 1$). The values of $[A]_0$ are indicated at the top of each section. Data for $[A]_0 = 0.03$ mM and $[A]_0 = 0.3$ mM are taken from Figures 4.17 and 4.19, respectively.

0.6 mL/h to 6 mL/h, the sharp repetitive signals obtained for A disappear and higher levels of S_1 are obtained.

Figure 4.30 shows the effect of the concentration of A in the feed stream, $[A]_0$, on the concentrations of S_1 and B when a CSTR is considered. It can seen that when the value of $[A]_0$ is increased from 0.03 mM to 0.3 mM, repetitive oscillatory signals are obtained. Similar effects are obtained when a PFR is considered, and these are shown in Figure 4.31. Moreover, the repetitive oscillatory signal is obtained after 100 min in a PFR, whereas in the CSTR it appears earlier, due to mixing in the reactor.

The effect of the maximum reaction rates, $V_{m,i}$, on the concentrations of S_1 and B when the CSTR is considered is presented in Figure 4.32. The concentration profile of B changes from constant concentration when $V_{m,i} = 0.1$ mM/min, to an oscillatory signal when $V_{m,i} = 0.2$ mM/min and to sharp on/off behavior when $V_{m,i} = 0.4$ mM/min. Similar characteristics of the signal can be seen in the concentration profiles of S_1. When the PFR is considered, increase in $V_{m,i}$ leads to effects resembling those shown in Figure 4.33. Here a time lag is observed in the concentration profiles of B and the period times for the on/off periods obtained when $V_{m,i} = 0.4$ mM/min are larger.

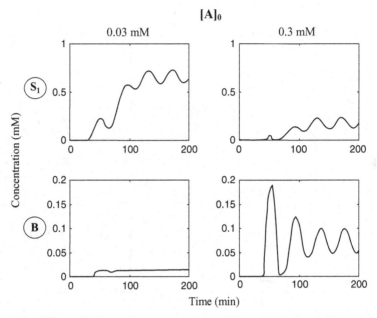

Figure 4.31 Effect of $[A]_0$ on the concentrations of S_1 and B in the basic system when operated as a PFR ($n = 5$). The values of $[A]_0$ are indicated at the top of each section. Data for $[A]_0 = 0.03$ mM and $[A]_0 = 0.3$ mM are taken from Figures 4.18 and 4.21, respectively.

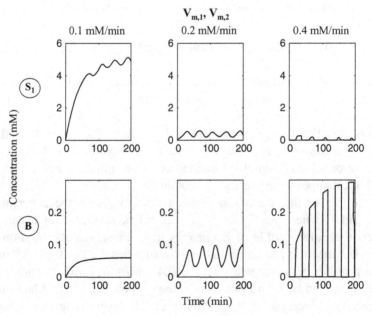

Figure 4.32 Effect of $V_{m,1}$ and $V_{m,2}$ (when $V_{m,1} = V_{m,2}$) on the concentrations of S_1 and B in the basic system when operated as a CSTR ($n = 1$). The values of $V_{m,1}$ and $V_{m,2}$ are indicated at the top of each section. Data for $V_{m,i} = 0.1$, 0.2, and 0.4 mM/min are taken from Figures 4.19, 4.22, and 4.24, respectively.

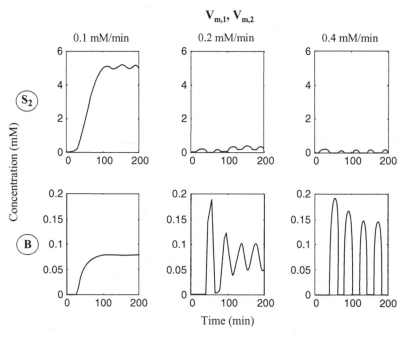

Figure 4.33 Effect of $V_{m,1}$ and $V_{m,2}$ (when $V_{m,1} = V_{m,2}$) on the concentrations of S_2 and B in the basic system when operated as a PFR ($n = 5$). The values of $V_{m,1}$ and $V_{m,2}$ are indicated at the top of each section. Data for $V_{m,i} = 0.1$, 0.2, and 0.4 mM/min are taken from Figures 4.23, 4.21, and 4.25, respectively.

The effect of the cycle time of the input signal, τ, on the concentrations of S_1 and B when the CSTR is considered is presented in Figure 4.34. It can be seen that for both S_1 and B the oscillatory signals obtained when $\tau = 20$ min are also observed when the value of τ is reduced to 5 min. However, for the PFR, as shown in Figure 4.35, the oscillatory behavior disappears when τ is reduced to 5 min.

b. Ping-Pong Mechanism, Internal Inhibition, and Product Inhibition   In the following numerical simulations, B and S_1 are considered as internal inhibitors in the basic system. Component B is inhibitory to enzyme E_1 (i.e., product inhibition) and component S_1 is inhibitory to enzyme E_2 (i.e., internal inhibition; see Section 4.1.3.2d). This situation is related to the experimental system described later (Section 4.3). In these cases, the rate of reaction (1) is expressed using equation (44) with $K_{i,B} = 0.027$ mM, and the rate of reaction (2) is expressed using equation (46). The sets of basic values used for the parameters involved are given in Table 4.3.

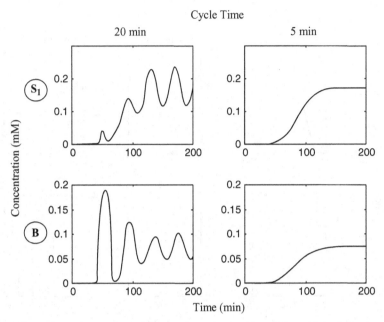

Figure 4.34   Effect of the cycle time (τ) on the concentrations of S_1 and B in the basic system when operated as a PFR ($n = 5$). The values of τ are indicated at the top of each section. Data for $\tau = 20$ min and $\tau = 5$ min are taken from Figures 4.21 and 4.27, respectively.

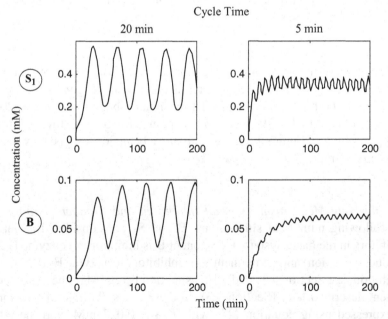

Figure 4.35   Effect of the cycle time (τ) on the concentrations of S_1 and B in the basic system when operated as a CSTR ($n = 1$). The values of τ are indicated on top of each section. Data for $\tau = 20$ min and $\tau = 5$ min are taken from Figures 4.19 and 4.26, respectively.

Table 4.3 Numerical Values of Operational Parameters Used in Simulations of a Packed Bed Reactor

Parameter	Symbol	Units	Value
Volume of the reactor	V	mL	7
Volumetric flow rate	Q	mL/h	ind.[a]
Cycle time	τ	min	5
Concentration range of S_1 in the feed stream	$S_{1,0}$	mM	1–10
Concentration range of S_2 in the feed stream	$S_{2,0}$	mM	1–10
Concentration of A in the feed stream	A_0	mM	0.3
Michaelis constant for S_1	K_{m,S_2}	mM	0.156
Michaelis constant for S_2	K_{m,S_1}	mM	0.0469
Michaelis constant for A	$K_{m,A}$	mM	0.076
Michaelis constant for B	$K_{m,B}$	mM	0.0266
Inhibition constant for S_1	K_{i,S_1}	mM	ind.[a]
Inhibition constant for B	$K_{i,B}$	mM	0.027
Maximal rate of the reaction $S_1 + A \rightarrow P_1 + B$	$V_{m,1}$	mM/min	0.5
Maximal rate of the reaction $S_2 + B \rightarrow P_2 + A$	$V_{m,2}$	mM/min	0.5

[a]ind.: indicated in the figure.

Figure 4.36 presents the effects of K_{i,S_1} on the concentration of B when three operation modes are considered for the reactor: CSTR, packed bed, and PFR. In all cases, increase in the value of K_{i,S_1} from 0.1 to 1 mM, meaning decreasing the inhibitory ability of S_1, causes a rather unexpected decrease in the concentrations of B, although B is a substrate of enzyme E_2, which is

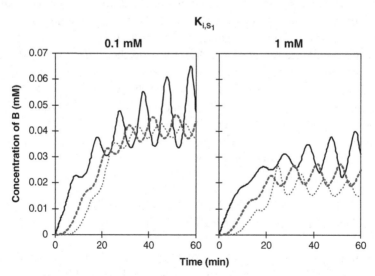

Figure 4.36 Effect of K_{i,S_1} on the concentration of B in the basic system when operated as a CSTR ($n = 1$, ———), packed bed reactor ($n = 3$, – – –), and PFR ($n = 5$, ······). Calculations were performed with the values of K_{i,S_1} indicated above and $Q = 20$ mL/h. The values used for all other parameters are given in Table 4.3.

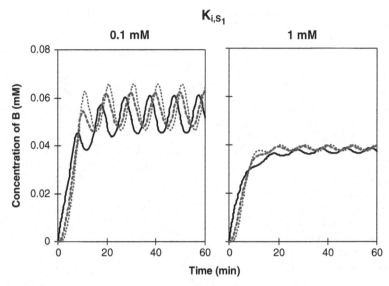

Figure 4.37 Effect of K_{i,S_1} on the concentration of B in the basic system when operated as CSTR ($n = 1$, ———), packed bed reactor ($n = 3$, – – –), and PFR ($n = 5$, $\cdots\cdots$). Calculations were performed with the values of K_{i,S_1} indicated above and $Q = 60$ mL/h. The values used for all other parameters are given in Table 4.3.

the enzyme inhibited by S_1. The coupling between the two reactions and the fact that B is also an inhibitor to enzyme E_1 make it difficult to predict the results, and this case emphasizes the absolute requirement for an analytical model such as the one developed here. The same phenomenon is observed in Figure 4.37, where the flow rate was increased to 60 mL/h.

In Figure 4.38 the effect of the flow rate and the inhibition constant K_{i,S_1} on the concentration of B is shown. In this figure data are taken from Figures 4.36 ($Q = 20$ mL/h) and 4.37 ($Q = 60$ mL/h), with $K_{i,S_1} = 0.1$ mM (left panel) and with $K_{i,S_1} = 1$ mM (right panel). In all cases the signals obtained are oscillatory with a time period of 10 min, which is also the time period of the input signal. However, various amplitudes and phase shifts are obtained when the parameters or the operational modes are changed.

4.2 NEURAL NETWORK–TYPE BIOCHEMICAL SYSTEMS FOR INFORMATION PROCESSING

Neural networks are systems built of basic, mutually interacting elements, called *neurons*. The two key features of a neural network model that are of interest to us here are the properties of each neuron and the connectivity between neurons. In this section the construction of biochemical networks

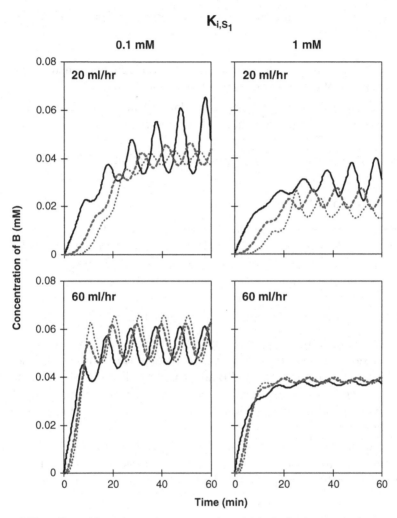

Figure 4.38 Effect of flow rate on the concentration of B in the basic system when operated as a CSTR ($n = 1$, ———), packed bed reactor ($n = 3$, – – –), and PFR ($n = 5$, $\cdots\cdots$). Calculations were performed with $K_{i,S_1} = 0.1$ mM (left panel) and $K_{i,S_1} = 1$ mM (right panel) and the values of Q indicated above. Data for $Q = 20$ and 60 mL/h are taken from Figures 4.36 and 4.37, respectively.

systems is discussed. In particular, these systems are proposed as "biochemical hardware" implementations of neural networks. In this study, the basic two-enzyme system discussed in Section 4.1 was chosen as the biochemical neuron. Also, connections between individual biochemical neurons are achieved by mass transfer: namely, by the flow of molecular species from one biochemical neuron to another. A defined array of such connections delineates the network characteristics.

In principle, there are two main possibilities for connecting biochemical neurons:

1. Chemical species that participate in one biochemical neuron can play the role of effector for another biochemical neuron.
2. Chemical species emerging as products from one neuron may be fed as substrates to a subsequent biochemical neuron.

Several examples studied are presented in Sections 4.2.1 to 4.2.4.

4.2.1 Network A

Network A, presented in Figure 4.39, is composed of n basic systems that operate simultaneously in a biochemical reactor and share cofactors A and B. The input to the network is made of $2n$ substrates, $S_1, S_2, S_3, \ldots, S_{2n}$ that are fed to the reactor at predetermined concentrations and rates.

4.2.1.1 Information-Processing Characteristics of Network A

Network A is designed to function as an information processor when each basic system can be seen as a node or a biochemical neuron in the network. In this network, cofactors A and B are shared by all the biochemical neurons of the network. Therefore, these biochemical neurons are fully connected to one another, and the information flows back and forth from each neuron to all others.

The input signal is composed of $2n$ concentration profiles of the partaking substrates. In this study it was considered that each of these concentration profiles either follows the pattern described in Figure 4.2 or is constant. The

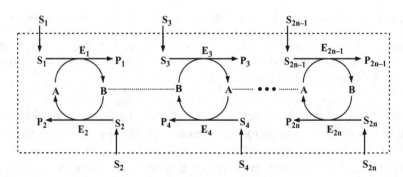

Figure 4.39   Network A. $S_1, S_2, \ldots, S_{2n}$: substrates; $P_1, P_2, \ldots, P_{2n}$: products; $E_1, E_2, \ldots,$ E_{2n}: participating enzymes; A, B: cofactors.

output signal is defined as the time course of concentration of any component in the network. Thus, this network can potentially produce $4n + 2$ output signals.

4.2.1.2 Analytical Model for Network A

Network A is built of n basic systems, and all the reactions take place in a fed-batch reactor. As such, the analytical model developed for network A is an extension of the model developed for the basic system (see Section 4.1.3.1). Based on the principles detailed in Section 4.1.3.1, the operational rules of network A are described by

$$\frac{d\,[S_i]}{dt} = \frac{Q}{V_0 + Qt}\,([S_i]_0 - [S_i]) - r_i \tag{49}$$

$$\frac{d\,[P_i]}{dt} = -\frac{Q}{V_0 + Qt}\,[P_i] + r_i \tag{50}$$

$$\frac{d\,[E_i]}{dt} = -\frac{Q}{V_0 + Qt}\,[E_i] \tag{51}$$

$$\frac{d\,[A]}{dt} = -\frac{Q}{V_0 + Qt}\,[A] - r_1 + r_2 + r_3 - r_4 - \cdots - r_{2n-1} + r_{2n} \tag{52}$$

$$\frac{d\,[B]}{dt} = -\frac{Q}{V_0 + Qt}\,[B] + r_1 - r_2 - r_3 + r_4 + \cdots + r_{2n-1} - r_{2n} \tag{53}$$

where i is the reaction number ($i = 1, 2, 3, 4, \ldots, 2n$) and r_i is the rate equation for reaction i.

Equations (49), (50), (52), and (53) are related to the reaction mechanism considered. In this case the mechanism considered is of the Ping-Pong type (see Section 4.1.3.1a), for which the rate equations are

$$r_i = \frac{V_{m,i}[S_i][A]}{K_{m,A}[S_i] + K_{m,S_i}[A] + [S_i][A]} \qquad i = 1, 4, 5, 8, 9, \ldots, 2n - 1 \tag{54}$$

$$r_i = \frac{V_{m,i}[S_i][B]}{K_{m,B}[S_i] + K_{m,S_i}[B] + [S_i][B]} \qquad i = 2, 3, 6, 7, 10, \ldots, 2n \tag{55}$$

Initial conditions for equations (49) to (53) are defined by the concentrations of substrates, products, and enzymes prevailing in the reactor at the onset of operation (at time $t = 0$):

$$
\begin{aligned}
[S_i] &= 0 \\
[P_i] &= 0 \\
[E_i] &= [E_i]_{t=0} \\
[A] &= [A]_{t=0} \\
[B] &= 0
\end{aligned}
\tag{56}
$$

where $i = 1, 2, 3, 4, \ldots, 2n$. Equations (49) to (53) are solved numerically according to the Runge–Kutta method [145] with the initial conditions defined in equation (56).

4.2.1.3   Results of Numerical Simulations for Network A

Calculations were performed for a network composed of two biochemical neurons (i.e., when two basic systems are operative). The various input signals and $V_{m,i}$ values considered are summarized in Table 4.4. All other parameter values are given in Table 4.5. Representative time courses are presented in Figures 4.40 to 4.43. In these figures, only the concentration profiles of S_1, S_2, S_3, S_4, A, and B are presented. These profiles were chosen due to their potential use as a result of information processing, and actually, each can be considered as the output signal. As mentioned for the basic system operated as a fed-batch reactor (Section 4.1.4.1), the concentration profiles of the reaction products do not have much meaning as a result of information processing, due to the fact that they accumulate in the reactor.

The characteristics of the output signals shown in Figure 4.40 are very similar to those obtained for the basic system (see Figure 4.4), so in this case the network has no advantage over a single basic system. This is also the case for the results presented in Figure 4.41. Here, the varied substrates in the feed are S_1 and S_3, and when compared to the results shown in Figure 4.40, it can

Table 4.4   Input Signal ($[S_1]_0$, $[S_2]_0$) and $V_{m,i}$ Used to Obtain Data in Figures 4.40 through 4.43[a]

Figure No.	n	$[S_1]_0$ (mM)	$[S_2]_0$ (mM)	$[S_3]_0$ (mM)	$[S_4]_0$ (mM)	$V_{m,1}$, $V_{m,2}$ (mM/min)	$V_{m,3}$, $V_{m,4}$ (mM/min)
40	2	/\/\	\/\/	45	45	0.4	0.4
41	2	/\/\	45	\/\/	45	0.4	0.4
42	2	/\/\	45	45	\/\/	0.4	0.4
43	2	/\/\	45	45	\/\/	0.7	0.1

[a] /\/\, \/\/: variable, following the profiles described in Section 4.1.2 and Figure 4.2.

Table 4.5 Numerical Values of Operational Parameters Used in Simulations of Biochemical Networks

Parameter	Symbol	Units	Value
Initial volume of the reaction mixture	V_0	mL	50
Volumetric flow rate	Q	mL/h	8
Cycle time	τ	min	5
Concentration range of S_i in the feed stream	$[S_i]_0$	mM	11–80
Initial concentration of A_i	$[A_i]_{t=0}$	mM	0.03
Michaelis constant for S_1	K_{m,S_1}	mM	0.036
Michaelis constant for S_2	K_{m,S_2}	mM	0.061
Michaelis constant for S_3	K_{m,S_3}	mM	0.036
Michaelis constant for S_4	K_{m,S_4}	mM	0.061
Michaelis constant for A_i	K_{m,A_i}	mM	0.0074
Michaelis constant for B_i	K_{m,B_i}	mM	0.0076

be seen that the output signal types follow this change, but they are still types obtained using the basic system alone.

The results obtained when the varied substrates in the feed are S_1 and S_4 are presented in Figure 4.42. It can be seen that in this case, the output signals obtained differ completely from those shown in Figures 4.40 and 4.41. The

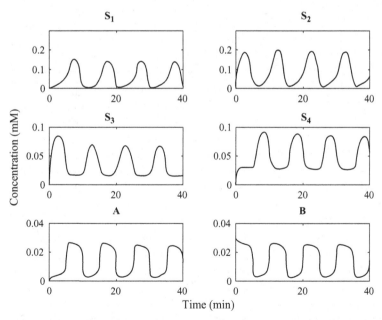

Figure 4.40 Time courses of concentrations of reactants in network A with $n = 2$. $[S_1]_0$ and $[S_2]_0$ are variable, $[S_3]_0$ and $[S_4]_0$ are constant, and the values of all parameters used are given in Table 4.5.

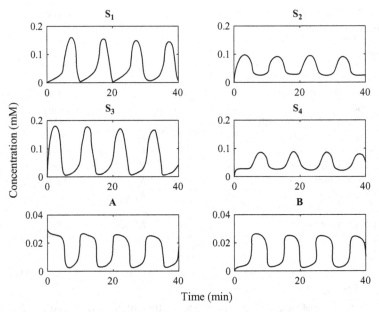

Figure 4.41   Time courses of concentrations of reactants in network A with $n = 2$. $[S_1]_0$ and $[S_3]_0$ are variable, $[S_2]_0$ and $[S_4]_0$ are constant, and the values of all parameters used are given in Table 4.5.

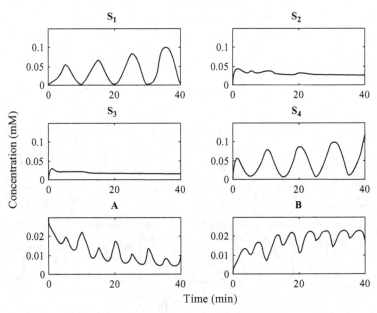

Figure 4.42   Time courses of concentrations of reactants in network A with $n = 2$. $[S_1]_0$ and $[S_4]_0$ are variable, $[S_2]_0$ and $[S_3]_0$ are constant, and the values of all parameters used are given in Table 4.5.

signals represented by the concentration profiles of S_1 and S_2 are similar to the input signals, and the signals represented by the concentration profiles of S_2 and S_3 are almost constant. However, the interesting signal is represented by the concentration profiles of A or B. These signals are characterized by a time period of 5 min (compared to 10 min in the input signal), and without intermediate periods of constant values. Thus, one can consider that the network performs an algebric operation, particularly division by 2. This result was not obtained with the basic system alone. Moreover, it was found that when higher values of n are considered, this signal is always obtained when the network is built of an even number of biochemical neurons and the variable substrates in the feed stream are S_1 and S_{2n}. When an odd number of biochemical neurons are connected in the network, the signals are of the type shown in Figures 4.40 and 4.41.

The results presented in Figure 4.43 were obtained with the same feed stream composition as for Figure 4.42, but for different values of $V_{m,i}$. Thus, the maximum reaction rates of the first biochemical neuron were increased from 0.4 mM/min to 0.7 mM/min, and the maximum reaction rates of the second biochemical neuron were reduced from 0.4 mM/min to 0.1 mM/min. It can be seen that the output signals obtained here are different from those

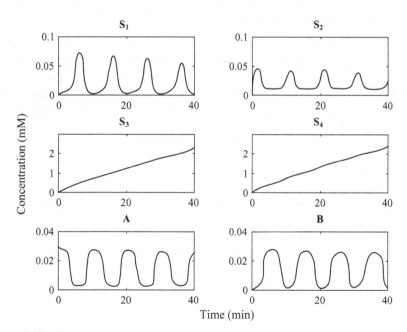

Figure 4.43 Time courses of concentrations of reactants in network A with $n = 2$. $[S_1]_0$ and $[S_4]_0$ are variable, $[S_2]_0$ and $[S_3]_0$ are constant, $V_{m,1} = V_{m,2} = 0.7$ mM/min, $V_{m,3} = V_{m,4} = 0.1$ mM/min, and the values of all other parameters used are given in Table 4.5.

obtained in Figure 4.42, and they are characterized by "on" and "off" periods similar to those in Figures 4.40 and 4.41. However, here the period times were 7 and 3 min, compared to the 5 min obtained in Figures 4.40 and 4.41.

As mentioned above, simulations were also carried out with higher values of n. However, the signals obtained in these simulations did not differ from those obtained with $n = 2$. Therefore, for the network system considered here, there is no advantage in employing more than two biochemical neurons in the network.

4.2.2   Network B

Network B, presented in Figure 4.44, is composed of n basic systems (the neurons) that operate in series (i.e., the products of one neuron are the substrates of the next one). The input to the system consists of the first two substrates, S_1 and S_2.

4.2.2.1   Information-Processing Characteristics of Network B

Network B is designed to operate as an information processor when each basic system functions as a node or a biochemical neuron in the network. In this network the information proceeds from one biochemical neuron to a subsequent neuron, but not in the opposite direction. Thus, the network is actually of the feedforward type.

The input signal consists of two concentration profiles of the substrates partaking, S_1 and S_2. In this study it was assumed that each of these concentration profiles can either follow the pattern described in Figure 4.2 or be constant. The output signal is defined as the time course of concentration of any component in the network. Thus, this network can potentially produce $4n + 2$ output signals.

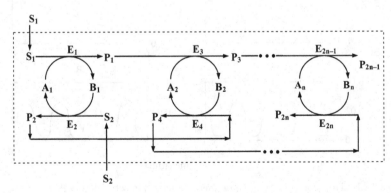

Figure 4.44   Network B. S_1, S_2: substrates; $P_1, P_2, \ldots, P_{2n}$: products and substrates; $E_1, E_2, \ldots, E_{2n}$: participating enzymes; $A_1, A_2, \ldots, A_n, B_1, B_2, \ldots, B_n$: cofactors.

4.2.2.2 Analytical Model for Network B

Network B is built of n basic systems, and all the reactions take place in a fed batch reactor. As such, the analytical model developed for network B is an extension of the model developed for the basic system (see Section 4.1.3.1). Based on the principles detailed in Section 4.1.3.1, the operational rules of network B are described by

$$\frac{d\,[S_i]}{dt} = \frac{Q}{V_0 + Qt}\left([S_i]_0 - [S_i]\right) - r_i \qquad i = 1, 2 \tag{57}$$

$$\frac{d\,[P_i]}{dt} = -\frac{Q}{V_0 + Qt}\,[P_i] + r_i - r_{i+2} \qquad i = 3, 4, 5, \ldots, 2n \tag{58}$$

$$\frac{d\,[E_i]}{dt} = -\frac{Q}{V_0 + Qt}\,[E_i] \qquad i = 1, 2, 3, \ldots, 2n \tag{59}$$

$$\frac{d\,[A_i]}{dt} = -\frac{Q}{V_0 + Qt}\,[A_i] - r_{2i-1} + r_{2i} \qquad i = 1, 2, 3, \ldots, n \tag{60}$$

$$\frac{d\,[B_i]}{dt} = -\frac{Q}{V_0 + Qt}\,[B_i] + r_{2i-1} - r_{2i} \qquad i = 1, 2, 3, \ldots, n \tag{61}$$

where n is the number of basic systems (biochemical neurons) in the network and r_i is the rate equation for the reaction catalyzed by E_i.

Equations (57), (58), (60), and (61) are related to the reaction mechanism considered. In this case the mechanism considered is of the ping-pong type (see Section 4.1.3.1a), for which the rate equations are

$$r_1 = \frac{V_{m,1}[S_1][A_1]}{K_{m,A_1}[S_1] + K_{m,S_1}[A_1] + [S_1][A_1]} \tag{62}$$

$$r_2 = \frac{V_{m,2}[S_2][B_1]}{K_{m,B_1}[S_2] + K_{m,S_2}[B_1] + [S_2][B_1]} \tag{63}$$

$$r_{2i-1} = \frac{V_{m,2i-1}[P_{2i-3}][A_i]}{K_{m,A_i}[P_{2i-3}] + K_{m,P_{2i-3}}[A_i] + [P_{2i-3}][A_i]} \qquad i = 2, 3, 4, \ldots, n \tag{64}$$

$$r_{2i} = \frac{V_{m,2i}[P_{2i-2}][B_i]}{K_{m,B_i}[P_{2i-2}] + K_{m,P_{2i-2}}[B_i] + [P_{2i-2}][B_i]} \qquad i = 2, 3, 4, \ldots, n \tag{65}$$

Initial conditions for equations (57) to (61) are defined by the concentrations of substrates, products, and enzymes prevailing in the reactor at the onset of operation (at time $t = 0$):

$$
\begin{aligned}
[S_i] &= 0 & i &= 1, 2 \\
[P_i] &= 0 & i &= 1, 2, 3, \ldots, 2n \\
[E_i] &= [E_i]_{t=0} & i &= 1, 2, 3, \ldots, 2n \\
[A_i] &= [A_i]_{t=0} & i &= 1, 2, 3, \ldots, n \\
[B_i] &= 0 & i &= 1, 2, 3, \ldots, n
\end{aligned}
\tag{66}
$$

Equations (57) to (61) are solved numerically according to the Runge–Kutta method [145] with initial conditions as defined in equation (66).

4.2.2.3   Results of Numerical Simulations for Network B

Representative results obtained from the numerical simulations performed for network B are presented below. The results collected in Figures 4.45 to 4.49 were obtained for a network composed of six biochemical neurons. The feedforward type of network has a particular characteristic. Thus, for neuron i in a network composed of n neurons (when $1 \leq i \leq n - 1$), the output signals of neuron i (i.e., P_{2i-1}, P_{2i}, A_i, and B_i), as well as A_n and B_n, are independent of n. Moreover, for such a network, the only outputs that depend on n are P_{2n-1} and P_{2n}. Thus, the only effect of adding neurons to the network is to increase the number of output signals available.

The concentration profiles of B_i are presented in Figures 4.45 to 4.49. They were chosen as representative of the information-processing capabilities of this type of network. Table 4.6 shows the parameters used to obtain the results reported in Figures 4.45 to 4.49. All other parameter values are given in Table 4.5. The values of the Michaelis constants were chosen as random numbers in the range 0.0001 to 0.1 mM for K_{m,S_i} and K_{m,P_i} and 0.0001 to 0.01 mM for K_{m,A_i} and K_{m,B_i}, and are detailed in Table 4.7.

Table 4.6   Input Signal ($[S_1]_0$, $[S_2]_0$), $K_{m,j}$, and $V_{m,i}$ Used to Obtain Data in Figures 4.45 through 4.49[a]

Figure No.	n	$[S_1]_0$ (mM)	$[S_2]_0$ (mM)	$K_{m,j}$ (mM)	$V_{m,i}$ (mM/min)
4.45	6	/\/\	\/\/	Set 1[b]	0.4
4.46	6	/\/\	\/\/	Set 2[b]	0.4
4.47	6	/\/\	\/\/	Set 1[b]	Various[c]
4.48	6	/\/\	\/\/	Set 2[b]	Various[c]
4.49	6	/\/\	45.5	Set 1[b]	0.4

[a]/\/\, \/\/: variable, following the profiles described in Section 4.1.2 and Figure 4.2.
[b]Values are given in Table 4.7.
[c]$V_{m,1} = V_{m,2} = 0.4$ mM, $V_{m,3} = V_{m,4} = 0.8$ mM, $V_{m,5} = V_{m,6} = 1.2$ mM, $V_{m,7} = V_{m,8} = 0.8$ mM, $V_{m,9} = V_{m,10} = 0.4$ mM, $V_{m,11} = V_{m,12} = 0.2$ mM.

Table 4.7 K_{m,S_i}, K_{m,P_i}, K_{m,A_i}, and K_{m,B_i} Used to Obtain Data in Figures 4.45 through 4.52

| | Set 1 | | | Set 2 | | |
| | | | | | | |
i	$K_{m,S_i} \times 10$ $K_{m,P_{i+2}} \times 10$	$K_{m,A_i} \times 10^2$	$K_{m,B_i} \times 10^2$	$K_{m,S_i} \times 10$ $K_{m,P_{i+2}} \times 10$	$K_{m,A_i} \times 10^2$	$K_{m,B_i} \times 10^2$
1	0.7012	0.3653	0.2470	0.2190	0.5297	0.6711
2	0.9103	0.9826	0.7227	0.0470	0.0077	0.3834
3	0.7622	0.7534	0.6515	0.6789	0.0668	0.4175
4	0.2625	0.0727	0.6316	0.6793	0.6868	0.5890
5	0.0475	0.8847	0.2727	0.9347	0.9304	0.8462
6	0.7361	0.0470	0.6793	0.3835	0.5194	0.8310
7	0.3282			0.5194		
8	0.6326			0.8310		
9	0.7564			0.0346		
10	0.9910			0.0535		
11	0.2190			0.9347		
12	0.6789			0.3835		

The results presented in Figure 4.45 were obtained with the $K_{m,j}$ values contained in set 1 of Table 4.7. In this case five types of output signals were found, and each is different from the input signal employed. Thus, the output signal represented by the concentration profile of B_1 is the one that is obtained when only one basic system is employed, and this is due to the fact that in

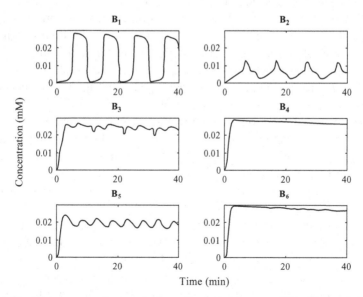

Figure 4.45   Time courses of concentrations of cofactors in network B with $n = 6$. $[S_1]_0$ and $[S_2]_0$ are variable, $V_{m,i} = 0.4$ mM/min, $K_{m,j}$ values are given in set 1 in Table 4.7, and the values of all other parameters used are given in Table 4.5.

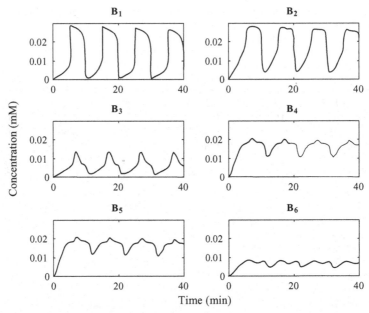

Figure 4.46   Time courses of concentrations of cofactors in network B with $n = 6$. $[S_1]_0$ and $[S_2]_0$ are variable, $V_{m,i} = 0.4$ mM/min, $K_{m,j}$ values are given in set 2 in Table 4.7, and the values of all other parameters used are given in Table 4.5.

a feedforward network each basic system is influenced only by those that precede and not by those that follow. The output signals represented by the concentration profiles of B_2 and B_3 show a repetitive complex signal with a period time of 10 min. This time period is the same as that of the input signal; thus, the information-processing here (i.e., represented by B_2 and B_3) causes a significant change in the signal type but not in the time period. The concentration profiles of B_4 and B_6 show an almost constant value. This is another type of information processing, but it can also be obtained when only one basic system is employed, and therefore B_4 and B_6 are not of much use. Of particular importance is output B_5. In this case a repetitive oscillatory signal with a time period of 5 min is obtained. Based on this observation, one can consider this network to be a "division machine," in which the input time period (i.e., 10 min) is divided by a factor of 2.

The results shown in Figure 4.46 were obtained for a network that differs from the preceding one only in the $K_{m,j}$ values. Here another set of random values was employed. It can be seen that altering the $K_{m,j}$ values from those used for data in Figure 4.45 led to completely different information-processing functions performed by the network. In this case three types of repetitive complex signals, with a time period of 10 min, were obtained. These are represented by the concentration profiles of B_3, B_4 (or B_5), and B_6.

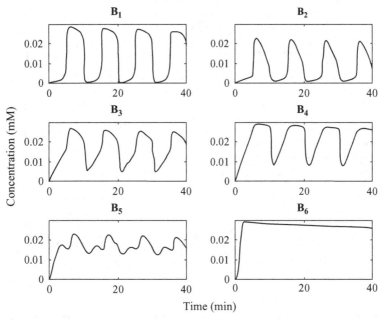

Figure 4.47   Time courses of concentrations of cofactors in network B with $n = 6$. $[S_1]_0$ and $[S_2]_0$ are variable, $V_{m,1} = V_{m,2} = 0.4$ mM, $V_{m,3} = V_{m,4} = 0.8$ mM, $V_{m,5} = V_{m,6} = 1.2$ mM, $V_{m,7} = V_{m,8} = 0.8$ mM, $V_{m,9} = V_{m,10} = 0.4$ mM, $V_{m,11} = V_{m,12} = 0.2$ mM, $K_{m,j}$ values are given in set 1 in Table 4.7, and the values of all other parameters used are given in Table 4.5.

The results presented in Figure 4.47 were obtained with values of $V_{m,i}$ which are different from those used for data in Figures 4.45 and 4.46. Comparing the results in Figure 4.47 to those presented in Figure 4.45 (where all the $V_{m,i}$ values were 0.4 mM), it can be seen that the output signals obtained in this case are affected by this change in $V_{m,i}$. Moreover, interesting results are presented by the concentration profile of B_5. This signal can be envisaged to be composed of two separate signals, each with a period time of 5 min but with different amplitudes. Therefore, in analogy to what was concluded for data on B_5 in Figure 4.45, one can also conclude that this network is a division machine in which the input signal is divided by a factor of 2.

The results shown in Figure 4.48 were obtained with a set of values similar to those used in Figure 4.47, the only difference being in the values of $K_{m,j}$. This change affects the performance of the network, and different information processing is achieved. Here, most of the signals are of the on/off type.

The results presented in Figure 4.49 were obtained when only one of the substrates is fed to the system with a variable concentration profile, while the second is constant. It can be seen that in this case, the performances obtained differ from those shown in Figures 4.45 to 4.48. The concentration

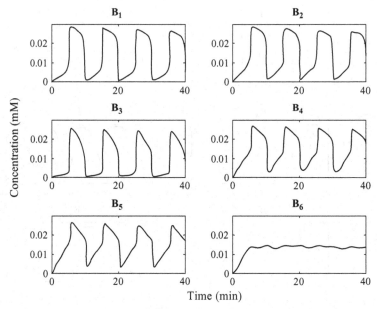

Figure 4.48   Time courses of concentrations of cofactors in network B with $n = 6$. $[S_1]_0$ and $[S_2]_0$ are variable, $V_{m,1} = V_{m,2} = 0.4$ mM, $V_{m,3} = V_{m,4} = 0.8$ mM, $V_{m,5} = V_{m,6} = 1.2$ mM, $V_{m,7} = V_{m,8} = 0.8$ mM, $V_{m,9} = V_{m,10} = 0.4$ mM, $V_{m,11} = V_{m,12} = 0.2$ mM, $K_{m,j}$ values are given in set 2 in Table 4.7, and the values of all other parameters used are given in Table 4.5.

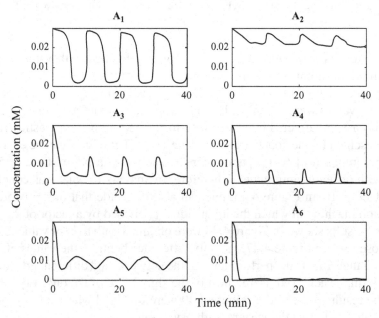

Figure 4.49   Time courses of concentrations of cofactors in network B with $n = 6$. $[S_1]_0$ is variable and $[S_2]_0$ is constant, $V_{m,i} = 0.4$ mM/min, $K_{m,j}$ values are given in set 1 in Table 4.7, and the values of all other parameters used are given in Table 4.5.

profile of A_3 shows a peak signal that appears every 14 min and lasts for 6 min. Moreover, the concentration profile of A_4 also shows a peak signal, but this one appears every 15 min and lasts for 5 min. These results imply that information-processing functions can also be achieved in this network when the input signal is less complex. Thus, data in Figure 4.49 can be interpreted to say that under these conditions, the network performs as a "pacemaker."

4.2.3 Network C

Network C, presented in Figure 4.50, is a variation of network B (Figure 4.44). In network B the cofactors for each basic system in the network are different. However, in network C all the basic systems in the network share cofactors A and B (i.e., $A_1 = A_2 = A_3 = \cdots = A_n = A$ and $B_1 = B_2 = B_3 = \cdots = B_n = B$).

4.2.3.1 Information-Processing Characteristics of Network C

In this network, the information proceeds from one biochemical neuron to a subsequent one and also in the opposite direction, and this is due to cofactors A and B, which are common to all the biochemical neurons in the network. Thus, this network is "fully connected" rather than being of the feedforward type exemplified by network B.

The input signal is composed of two concentration profiles of the substrates partaking, S_1 and S_2. In this study it was assumed that each concentration profile either follows the pattern described in Figure 4.2, or is constant. The output signal is defined as the time course of concentration of any component in the network. Thus, this network can potentially produce $2n + 4$ output signals.

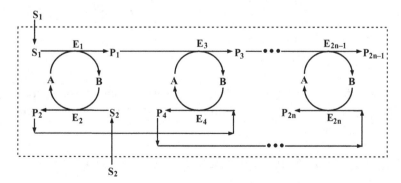

Figure 4.50   Network C. S_1, S_2: substrates; P_1, P_2, ..., P_{2n}: products and substrates; E_1, E_2, ..., E_{2n}: participating enzymes; A, B: cofactors.

4.2.3.2   Analytical Model for Network C

The analytical model developed for network C assumes that the reactions take place in a fed-batch reactor and is a variation of the model developed for network B (see Section 4.2.2.2). Equations (57) to (59), written for network B, are valid here as well. In addition, the mass balances of the cofactors A and B are given by

$$\frac{d\,[\text{A}]}{dt} = -\frac{Q}{V_0 + Qt}\,[\text{A}] - r_1 + r_2 - r_3 + r_4 - \cdots - r_{2n-1} + r_{2n} \quad (67)$$

$$\frac{d\,[\text{B}]}{dt} = -\frac{Q}{V_0 + Qt}\,[\text{B}] + r_1 - r_2 + r_3 - r_4 + \cdots + r_{2n-1} - r_{2n} \quad (68)$$

where n is the number of basic systems (biochemical neurons) in the network and r_i is the rate equation for the reaction catalyzed by E_i.

Equations (57) to (59), (67), and (68) are related to the reaction mechanism considered, in this case is the ping-pong type (see Section 4.1.3.1a), and the rate equations are

$$r_i = \frac{V_{m,i}[\text{P}_{i-2}][\text{A}]}{K_{m,\text{A}}[\text{P}_{i-2}] + K_{m,\text{P}_{i-2}}[\text{A}] + [\text{P}_{i-2}][\text{A}]} \qquad i = 3, 5, 7, \ldots, 2n - 1 \quad (69)$$

$$r_i = \frac{V_{m,i}[\text{P}_{i-2}][\text{B}]}{K_{m,\text{B}}[\text{P}_{i-2}] + K_{m,\text{P}_{i-2}}[\text{B}] + [\text{P}_{i-2}][\text{B}]} \qquad i = 4, 6, 8, \ldots, 2n \quad (70)$$

Initial conditions for equations (57) to (59), (67), and (68) are defined by the concentrations of the substrates, products, and enzymes in the reactor at the onset of operation (at time $t = 0$):

$$\begin{aligned}
[\text{S}_i] &= 0 & i &= 1, 2 \\
[\text{P}_i] &= 0 & i &= 1, 2, 3, \ldots, 2n \\
[\text{E}_i] &= [\text{E}_i]_{t=0} & i &= 1, 2, 3, \ldots, 2n \\
[\text{A}] &= [\text{A}]_{t=0} \\
[\text{B}] &= 0
\end{aligned} \qquad (71)$$

Equations (57) to (59), (67), and (68) are solved numerically according to the Runge–Kutta method [145] with initial conditions as defined in equation (71).

4.2.3.3   Results of Numerical Simulations for Network C

Representative results obtained from the numerical simulations performed for network C are presented below. The results collected in Figures 4.51 to

Table 4.8 Input Signal ($[S_1]_0$, $[S_2]_0$) and $K_{m,j}$ Used to Obtain Data in Figures 4.51 through 4.53[a]

Figure No.	n	$[S_1]_0$ (mM)	$[S_2]_0$ (mM)	$K_{m,j}$ (mM)
4.51	3	/\/\	\/\/	Set 1[b]
4.52	4	/\/\	\/\/	Set 1[b]
4.53	6	/\/\	\/\/	Set 1[b]

[a] /\/\, \/\/: variable, following the profiles in Section 4.1.2 and Figure 4.2.
[b] Values are given in Table 4.7.

4.53 were obtained for a network composed of three, four, and six biochemical neurons, respectively. This network is fully connected, and therefore the results depend on the number of biochemical neurons connected. Representative concentration profiles are presented in Figures 4.51 to 4.53. Table 4.8 summarizes the number of biochemical neurons in the network, the input signal compositions, and the $K_{m,j}$ values employed to obtain the results in Figures 4.51 to 4.53. All other parameter values are given in Table 4.5. The $K_{m,j}$ values are random numbers as detailed in Table 4.7.

The results presented in Figure 4.51 were obtained for a network composed of three basic systems, and representative concentration profiles are shown. It

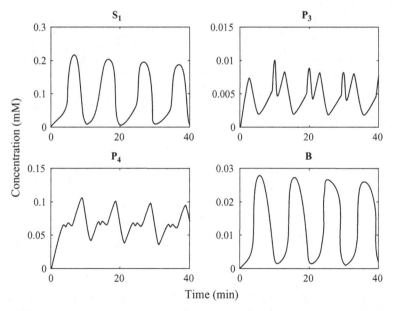

Figure 4.51 Time courses of concentrations of reactants in network C with $n = 3$. $[S_1]_0$ and $[S_2]_0$ are variable, $V_{m,i} = 0.4$ mM/min, $K_{m,j}$ values follow set 1 in Table 4.7, and the values of all other parameters used are given in Table 4.5.

can be seen that the signal type represented by the concentration profiles of S_1 and B had already been obtained in other simulations (e.g., in the basic system, Section 4.1.4). Of particular interest is the concentration profile of P_3. This is a repetitive signal with a time period of 10 min, but each 10-min period can be subdivided into two different signal types, each of which is characterized by a time period of 5 min. Thus, division by 2 is also performed by this network. A similar case is that of the signal represented by the concentration profile of P_4. A repetitive signal with a time period of 10 min is obtained. This 10-min period can be subdivided into three periods, two of 2.5 min each and one of 5 min. Thus, the network performs a combination of division by 2 and by 4.

The results obtained when the network was operated with four neurons are presented in Figure 4.52. It can be seen that the concentration profiles of S_1 and B are of the same type as those obtained in Figure 4.51 when $n = 3$. However, a completely different profile is obtained for P_4, for which a repetitive signal with a time period of 5 min is observed. Thus, this system also performs a division by 2 operation. The concentration profile of P_3 is a repetitive signal with a time period of 10 min, but each 10-min period can be subdivided into two different signal types, each of which is characterized by

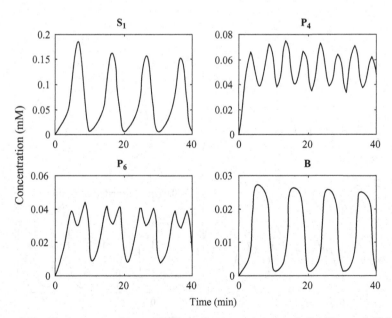

Figure 4.52 Time courses of concentrations of reactants in network C with $n = 4$. $[S_1]_0$ and $[S_2]_0$ are variable, $V_{m,i} = 0.4$ mM/min, $K_{m,j}$ values follow set 1 in Table 4.7, and the values of all other parameters used are given in Table 4.5.

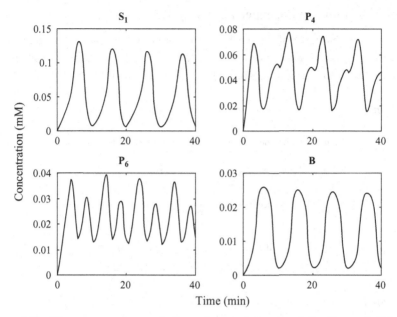

Figure 4.53   Time courses of concentrations of reactants in network C with $n = 6$. $[S_1]_0$ and $[S_2]_0$ are variable, $V_{m,i} = 0.4$ mM/min, $K_{m,j}$ values follow set 1 in Table 4.7, and the values of all other parameters used are given in Table 4.5.

a time period of 5 min. Therefore, here again division by 2 is performed by the network.

The results presented in Figure 4.53 were obtained with six biochemical neurons in the network. In this case the types of signal obtained are very similar to those in Figure 4.52. A repetitive signal with a time period of 5 min (that means division by 2) is obtained for P_6. The concentration profile of P_4 is a repetitive signal with a period of 10 min that can be subdivided into two different signal types, each of which is characterized with a time period of 5 min. Therefore, with respect to these profiles, division by 2 is performed by this network as well.

4.3   THE BASIC SYSTEM: EXPERIMENTAL RESULTS

The basic system was introduced and defined in Sections 4.1.1 and 4.1.2, and pertinent analytical models for various operation modes were described in Section 4.1.3. In this section an experimental interpretation of the basic system is introduced, and the experimental results are investigated in terms of the analytical models developed in Section 4.1.3.

4.3.1   Deciding on the experimental system

To assess the validity of the analytical model developed for the basic system as well as of the results of pertinent numerical simulations, three experimental systems were investigated as model systems. These are presented below.

System 1

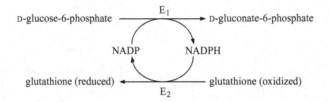

where E_1 = glucose-6-phosphate-dehydrogenase (G6PDH, E.C. 1.1.1.49)
E_2 = glutathione reductase (GR, E.C. 1.6.4.2)

System 2

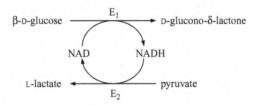

where E_1 = glucose dehydrogenase (GDH, E.C. 1.1.1.47)
E_2 = L-lactate dehydrogenase (LDH, E.C. 1.1.1.27)

System 3

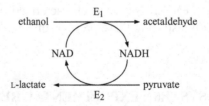

where E_1 = alcohol dehydrogenase (ADH, E.C. 1.1.1.1)
E_2 = L-lactate dehydrogenase (LDH, E.C. 1.1.1.27)

The experimental system was selected based on the conclusions obtained from numerical simulations. Thus, in Section 4.1.4.1a it was found that to obtain an on/off output signal in a fed-batch reactor, the values of $V_{m,1}$ and

Table 4.9 Values of $K_{m,j}$ Determined for Substrates of Experimental Systems

System No.	Enzyme	Source	Buffer	Substrate	$K_{m,j}$ (mM) Experimental	$K_{m,j}$ (mM) Literature[a]
1	G6PDH	*Torula* yeast	Tris, 0.1 M, pH 8, 10 mM MgCl$_2$, 0.94 mM EDTA	G6P NADP	0.156 0.076	0.23 0.067
	GR	Baker's yeast	Tris, 0.1 M, pH 8, 10 mM MgCl$_2$, 0.94 mM EDTA	GSSG NADPH	0.047 0.027	0.061 0.0076
2	GDH	*Bacillus megaterium*	Phosphate, 0.1 M, pH 7.55	Glucose NAD	22.1 0.26	47.5 4.5
2,3	LDH	Rabbit muscle	Phosphate, 0.1 M, pH 7.55	Pyruvate NADH	0.575 0.055	0.164 0.011
3	ADH	Baker's yeast	Phosphate, 0.1 M, pH 7.55	Ethanol NAD	99.98 0.934	26 0.108

[a]The values of $K_{m,j}$ taken from the literature were not always obtained using the same experimental conditions as those employed in this work. For details, see Table 1.4 in Section 1.6.

$V_{m,2}$ should be about 20 times the value of the largest $K_{m,j}$ value in the system. As such, relatively large amounts of enzymes are needed in each operation. (It should be pointed out that in the basic system, the two reactions take place simultaneously in the same medium and therefore the reaction conditions are not always optimal for both enzymes.) Thus, to examine the possibility of using the systems suggested above as experimental systems, the values of $K_{m,j}$ had to be determined for each of the substrates involved and under the experimental conditions actually employed. The results obtained are presented in Table 4.9. From these values the amounts of enzymes needed for each operation were estimated.

From the results presented in Table 4.9 it can be seen that in systems 2 and 3, the substrates involved (i.e., glucose and ethanol) are characterized by high K_m constants. High K_m values for these substrates are also indicated in the literature. Only in system 1 do both reactions involve moderate values of $K_{m,j}$ and so can be operated with reasonable amounts of enzymes. Thus, system 1 was chosen to represent the basic system.

4.3.2 Kinetic Study of the Experimental System

The development and use of appropriate analytical models require not only knowledge of the kinetic parameters involved but also of the mechanisms of the participating reactions. As such, the studies performed addressed both these aspects.

4.3.2.1 Kinetic Parameters and Mechanism of a Reaction Catalyzed by G6PDH

The reaction considered is

$$\text{D-gluscose-6-phosphate} + \text{NADP} \xrightarrow{\text{G6PDH}} \text{D-gluconate-6-phosphate} + \text{NADPH}$$

The kinetic characteristics of this reaction were studied according to the procedure described in Section 3.3.1.4. The results obtained are presented in Figure 4.54 in terms of Lineweaver–Burk reciprocal plots. The intercepts and slopes of the lines shown in Figure 4.54 are plotted in Figure 4.55.

From Figure 4.54 it can be seen that the family of reciprocal plots obtained at different fixed concentrations of NADP are essentially parallel to one another. This is also indicated in Figure 4.55, where the value of the slopes of the lines seem to be approximately constant. These results imply that the velocity equation for the ping-pong mechanism [146] can be used to describe the rate of the reaction catalyzed by G6PDH. Although initial velocity studies alone cannot define the exact kinetic mechanism [146,147], we are more interested in the appropriate rate equation that describes the reaction progress.

From the replots presented in Figure 4.55, the values of $K_{m,j}$ of the substrates D-glucose-6-phosphate and NADP can be determined. In this case the slope is constant and equals $K_{m,\text{G6P}}/V_{\max}$. Furthermore, the line obtained from the intercepts replot is defined by the following parameters: slope = $K_{m,\text{NADP}}/V_{\max}$ and intercept = $1/V_{\max}$. From these slopes and intercepts the values obtained for $K_{m,j}$ are $K_{m,\text{G6P}} = 0.156$ mM and $K_{m,\text{NADP}} = 0.076$ mM.

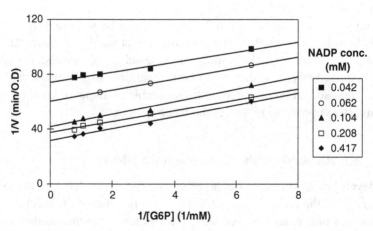

Figure 4.54 $1/V$ versus $1/[G6P]$ at various initial concentrations of NADP.

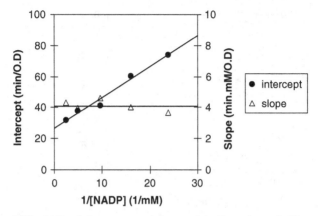

Figure 4.55 $1/V$ axis intercepts and slopes of the lines shown in Figure 4.54.

4.3.2.2   Kinetic Parameters for a Reaction Catalyzed by GR

The reaction considered is

$$GSSG + NADPH \xrightarrow{\quad GR \quad} 2GSH + NADP$$

The kinetic characteristics of this reaction were studied according to the procedure described in Section 3.3.1.5. The results obtained are presented in Figure 4.56 in terms of Lineweaver–Burk reciprocal plots. The intercepts and slopes of the lines shown in Figure 4.56 are plotted in Figure 4.57.

From Figure 4.56 it can be seen that the family of reciprocal plots obtained at different fixed concentrations of NADPH are essentialy parallel to one another. This is also indicated in Figure 4.57, where the value of the slopes

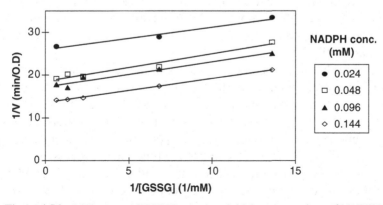

Figure 4.56 $1/V$ versus $1/[GSSG]$ at various initial concentrations of NADPH.

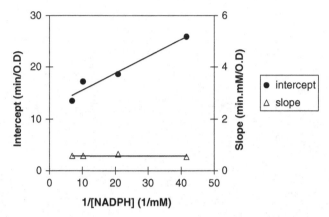

Figure 4.57 $1/V$ axis intercepts and slopes of the lines shown in Figure 4.56.

of the lines seem to be approximately constant. These results imply that the reaction proceeds by the ping-pong mechanism [146].

From the replots presented in Figure 4.57, the values of $K_{m,j}$ of the substrates glutathione (oxidized) and NADPH can be determined. In this case the slope is constant and equals $K_{m,\text{GSSG}}/V_{\text{max}}$. Furthermore, the line obtained from the intercepts replot is defined by the following parameters: slope = $K_{m,\text{NADPH}}/V_{\text{max}}$ and intercept = $1/V_{\text{max}}$. From these slopes and intercepts the values obtained for $K_{m,j}$ are $K_{m,\text{GSSG}} = 0.0469$ mM and $K_{m,\text{NADPH}} = 0.0266$ mM.

4.3.3 Control of the Input Signal

The input signal entering the experimental system is actually continuous changes in the concentrations of one or two compounds that are fed to the reactor. However, the concentration profiles of these compounds follow the function described in Section 4.1.2. To achieve the desired concentration profiles in the experimental system, the flow rates of the feed streams are computer controlled.

In this study the concentration profiles in the feed stream are delineated prior to operation, and these profiles are interpreted in terms of the flow rates of the two entering streams. Thus, the compounds that are fed at variable concentrations are each present in one vessel, and two peristaltic pumps flow these compounds to the reactor. The peristaltic pumps are computer controlled and change their flow rate according to the function in process.

Control of the peristaltic pumps is achieved using a DT 2811-PGH data acquisition board and a program written for the specific case. The card enables ordering predesigned flow-rate profiles to the pumps and reports the actual performance of the pumps. To operate the control system the input required in the software is composed of the following data:

- The minimum and maximum flow rates of each pump
- The cycle time for each pump
- The total time of the experiment

Using these data the flow-rate profiles are calculated and the information is transfered to the peristaltic pump.

4.3.4   The Basic System in a Fed-Batch Reactor

The basic system containing the enzymes G6PDH and GR was operated in a fed-batch reactor, and this experimental system is shown schematically in Figure 4.58. In this system the enzymes and the cofactor NADP are present in the reactor before the onset of operation and the substrates G6P and GSSG are fed into the system at predetermined concentration profiles. The peristaltic pumps P1 and P2 are computer controlled and produce modified variable flow rates between 1 and 6 mL/h, with a cycle time of 5 min. However, at the reactor inlet the combined flow rate is always 7 mL/h and the concentrations of the substrates, G6P and GSSG, vary between 13.3 and 80 mM. The output signal of the system is represented by the time-dependent concentration profile of NADPH. To measure the concentration of NADPH, the reaction mixture is circulated rapidly, using peristaltic pump P3, through a spectrophotometer flow-through cell where the optical density is measured continuously at 339 nm and recorded using the recorder attached.

To avoid massive dilution of the reaction mixture in the fed-batch reactor, the initial reactor volume was rather large relative to the flow rate of the feed streams. However, the initial volume of the reactor affects the amounts of enzymes that are required. As shown in Section 4.1.4.1, large amounts of enzymes are needed for each volume unit in the reactor, and in order to work with reasonable amounts of enzymes, this volume was limited to 50 mL.

The initial volume of 50 mL chosen for the fed-batch reactor imposes relatively low flow rates for the feed stream, as indicated above. However, variations in the concentrations of the substrates in the feed stream are based on variations in the flow rates, and these should be accurate. These considerations lead to a need for accurate changes in a limited range of flow rates. The flow rate of 7 mL/h is in the lowest range of the rates defined by the producer for the peristaltic pumps used, so in the settings defined by the producer, accurate variations could not be obtained. Thus, the peristaltic pumps were operated with tubings of very small diameter. These tubings, of 0.5 mm inner

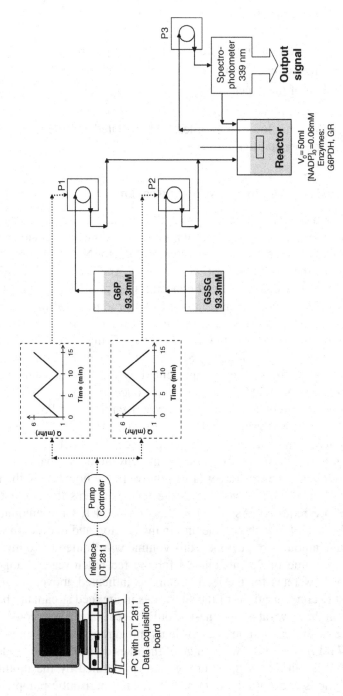

Figure 4.58 Experimental configuration employed for operation of the basic system in a fed-batch reactor. (.....): control lines; (---): input information; (—): fluid flow lines; P1, P2, P3: peristaltic pumps; G6P: glucose-6-phosphate; GSSG: oxidized glutathione.

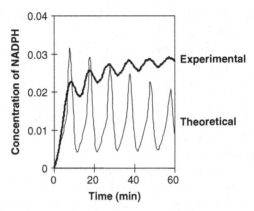

Figure 4.59 Experimental and theoretical results obtained for the basic system using G6PDH and GR, and operated as a fed-batch reactor. Results were obtained with $V_{m,\text{G6PDH}} = V_{m,\text{GR}} = 0.5$ mM/min.

diameter, were not defined by the producer, and their use required special fittings and calibration of the pumps.

Delineation of the operational parameters was achieved using computer simulations as described in Section 4.1.3.1. The values of $K_{m,j}$ (determined experimentally), the initial reactor volume, and the initial concentration of NADP were fed into the program. Employing the conclusions obtained from the theoretical simulations, the other parameters (i.e., flow rates, concentration range of the substrates, and $V_{m,i}$ values) were calculated according to the output signal desired.

Figure 4.59 presents the results obtained when the basic system, containing G6PDH and GR, was operated as a fed-batch reactor in the configuration described in Figure 4.58. For comparison, the results of pertinent numerical simulations are also shown. It can be seen that the signal obtained in the experimental system indeed follows the characteristic course shown by the signal calculated, but the actual numerical values are different. This dissimilarity has been attributed to inhibition effects in the reactions involved, effects that were not considered in the calculations. Therefore, a search for potential inhibitors was undertaken.

4.3.5   Internal Inhibition in the Basic System

Based on the results of the preceding section, potential inhibitors to the enzymes involved, G6PDH and GR, were searched for among the compounds that participate in the experimental system considered. It was found that GR is inhibited by G6P, the substrate of the other reaction. To determine the inhibition constant, G6P was considered as a dead-end inhibitor [146] that affects a reaction proceeding by the ping-pong mechanism. The rate equation for this case is indicated in Section 4.1.3.2d.

The value of $K_{i,G6P}$ was evaluated from results of separate experiments in which GR catalyzes the reduction of GSSG by NADPH in the presence of various concentrations of G6P as inhibitor. The procedure employed is described in Section 3.3.2, and the pertinent results, plotted as $1/V$ versus $1/[GSSG]$, are presented in Figure 4.60. It can be seen that whenever the inhibitor G6P is present, the lines bend upward as they approach the $1/V$ axis. This bend becomes more pronounced as the concentration of G6P increases. This behavior is usually associated with substrate inhibition [149] and perhaps the inhibitor G6P affects the substrate GSSG and the latter becomes inhibitory to the enzyme GR. However, this effect was not considered in the rate equations used in the experimental system.

The straight lines obtained for large values of $1/[GSSG]$ were extrapolated to the $1/V$ axis to determine the inhibition constant, and this procedure is presented in Figure 4.61. The lines in Figure 4.61 are close to parallel, and we can conclude that the inhibitor and the varied substrate (GSSG) combine with different enzyme forms [146]. Thus, G6P competes with NADPH and the value of $K_{i,G6P}$ can be determined from the intercept replot presented in Figure 4.62. From the slope of the line obtained in Figure 4.62, $K_{i,G6P}$ is evaluated as 8.4 mM.

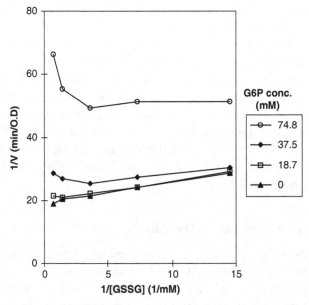

Figure 4.60 $1/V$ versus $1/[GSSG]$ plot at different fixed concentrations of the inhibitor G6P and a constant concentration of NADPH.

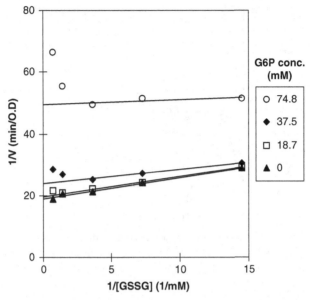

Figure 4.61 $1/V$ versus 1/[GSSG] plot at different fixed concentrations of the inhibitor G6P and a constant concentration of NADPH. This plot is similar to Figure 4.60 except that the straight lines were extrapolated to 1/[GSSG] → 0.

4.3.6   Prediction of the Analytical Model Considering Internal Inhibition in a Fed-Batch Reactor

Based on the conclusions drawn in Section 4.3.5, the theoretical results presented in Figure 4.59 were recalculated, now taking the inhibition of GR by G6P into consideration. The results of such calculations, using various values for $K_{i,\text{G6P}}$, are presented in Figure 4.63. In this figure the experimental

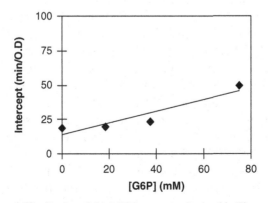

Figure 4.62   Replot of the $1/V$ intercepts obtained in Figure 4.61.

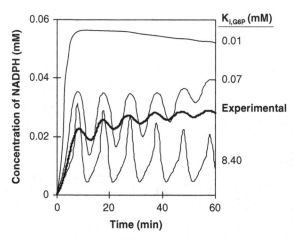

Figure 4.63 Experimental and theoretical results obtained for the basic system with G6PDH and GR when operated as a fed-batch reactor. Theoretical results were obtained considering G6P as an inhibitor to GR and with $V_{m,G6PDH} = V_{m,GR} = 0.5$ mM/min.

results shown in Figure 4.59 were also included. It can be seen that consideration of the internal inhibition indeed affects the output signal, and the results obtained from the analytical model are in better agreement with the experimental results than when inhibition was neglected. However, this improvement is achieved for inhibition constants that are much smaller than the value of 8.4 mM found experimentally.

A more detailed analysis of these results is presented in Figure 4.64. Here the experimental results presented in Figure 4.63 are shown again, and numerical simulations carried out using inhibition constants that are close to 0.07 mM are also presented. It can again be seen that none of the theoretical results agree fully with the experimental concentration profile.

To investigate these systems in an even more detailed manner, consideration was given to additional experimental findings. Thus, in previous studies it was shown that NADPH is inhibitory to the enzyme G6PDH and competes with NADP [132]. For this system, an inhibition constant of 0.027 mM was calculated [132]. This inhibition process was now added to the numerical simulation performed for our system, and new calculations were performed considering both the inhibition of GR by G6P and of G6PDH by NADPH. The results obtained are shown in Figure 4.65. It can be seen that in this case good agreement between the experimental and theoretical results is obtained when $K_{i,G6P} = 0.15$ mM and $K_{i,NADPH} = 0.027$ mM.

Results of additional studies are presented in Figure 4.66. These results were also obtained in a fed-batch reactor, but in this case different $V_{m,i}$ values were employed: namely, $V_{m,G6PDH} = 0.211$ mM/min and

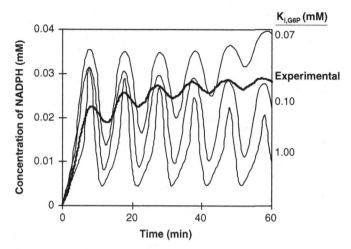

Figure 4.64 Experimental and theoretical results obtained for the basic system with G6PDH and GR when operated as a fed-batch reactor. Theoretical results were obtained considering G6P as an inhibitor to GR and with $V_{m,\text{G6PDH}} = V_{m,\text{GR}} = 0.5$ mM/min.

$V_{m,\text{GR}} = 0.136$ mM/min. In Figure 4.66 theoretical results obtained from the analytical model without considering inhibition of G6PDH by NADPH are also presented. It can be seen that when inhibition by G6P was not considered in the analytical model ($K_{i,\text{G6P}} = \infty$), the theoretical results are very different from the experimental results. This agreement improves when inhibition

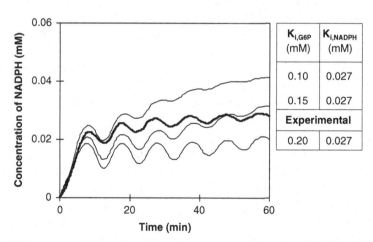

Figure 4.65 Experimental and theoretical results obtained for the basic system with G6PDH and GR when operated as a fed-batch reactor. Theoretical results were obtained with $V_{m,\text{G6PDH}} = V_{m,\text{GR}} = 0.5$ mM/min and considering G6P as an inhibitor of GR and NADPH as an inhibitor of G6PDH with the inhibition constants indicated above.

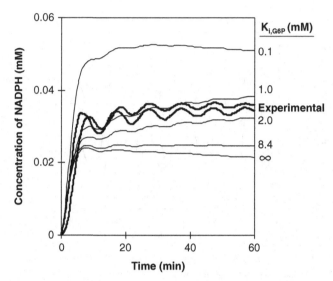

Figure 4.66 Experimental and theoretical results obtained for the basic system using G6PDH and GR and operated as a fed-batch reactor. Theoretical results were obtained with $V_{m,\text{G6PDH}} = 0.211$ mM/min and $V_{m,\text{GR}} = 0.136$ mM/min and considering G6P as an inhibitor to GR with the indicated values of $K_{i,\text{G6P}}$ (∞ = no inhibition by G6P). No inhibition of G6PDH by NADPH is considered here.

by G6P is considered in the analytical model. As obtained for the previous experiment (Figures 4.63 to 4.65), good agreement is accomplished with $K_{i,\text{G6P}}$ values that are smaller than that obtained experimentally (8.4 mM). However, in this case the $K_{i,\text{G6P}}$ value that leads to the best agreement is close to 1 mM.

An additional step along this line was taken when inhibition of the enzyme G6PDH by NADPH and that of GR by G6P were both considered in the numerical simulations. The results obtained are presented in Figure 4.67. It can be seen that in this case the experimental results lay between the theoretical results obtained with $K_{i,\text{G6P}} = 0.15$ mM and $K_{i,\text{G6P}} = 1$ mM. These values are close to the $K_{i,\text{G6P}}$ value that gave the best fit in the previous case (Figure 4.65), 0.15 mM. However, the value that was determined experimentally for $K_{i,\text{G6P}}$ is larger and equals 8.4 mM. This difference can be caused by the existence of additional processes that were not taken into account in the analytical model and they are therefore expressed in the value of $K_{i,\text{G6P}}$. For example, the effect observed in Section 4.3.5, where it was suggested that GSSG becomes inhibitory to the enzyme GR in the presence of G6P, was not considered.

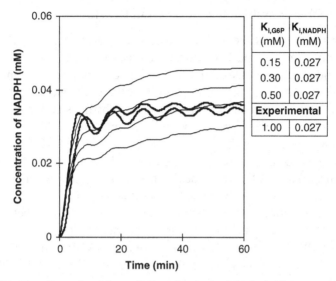

$K_{i,G6P}$ (mM)	$K_{i,NADPH}$ (mM)
0.15	0.027
0.30	0.027
0.50	0.027
Experimental	
1.00	0.027

Figure 4.67   Experimental and theoretical results obtained for the basic system with G6PDH and GR when operated as a fed-batch reactor. Theoretical results were obtained with $V_{m,G6PDH} = 0.211$ mM/min and $V_{m,GR} = 0.136$ mM/min and considering G6P as an inhibitor of GR and NADPH as an inhibitor of G6PDH with the inhibition constants indicated above.

4.3.7   Immobilization of G6PDH and GR

Immobilization of the enzymes G6PDH and GR on Affi-Gel 10 was carried out according to the procedure described in Section 3.3.3. The enzymes were immobilized separately and the results of the immobilization processes are summarized in Table 4.10. It can be seen that even though large amounts of the enzymes were immobilized on the gel, only a small fraction remained active after immobilization. This is probably related to steric hindrance caused by the immobilized proteins. The procedure in which incubation was carried out for 24 h at 4°C gave better results in means of the immobilized enzyme activity. Therefore, gels containing the immobilized enzymes obtained in this batch were mixed together and packed in the reactor.

Table 4.10   Results Obtained in Immobilization of G6PDH and GR on Affi-Gel 10

Enzyme	Incubation conditions	Immobilized Units (%)	Active Units (%)
G6PDH	1 h at room temp	57	0.4
GR	1 h at room temp	63	0.7
G6PDH	24 h at 4°C	61	1.2
GR	24 h at 4°C	42	7.8

4.3.8   The Basic System in a Packed Bed Reactor

In this part of the study the basic system containing the enzymes G6PDH and GR was operated as a packed bed reactor rather than the fed-batch type of reactor studied in Sections 4.3.4 to 4.3.6. The experimental system is shown schematically in Figure 4.68. In this system the gel containing both immobilized enzymes is packed in the reactor. The substrates G6P and GSSG and are fed into the system at predetermined concentration profiles. The cofactor NADP is also present in the feed stream, but it is fed in a constant concentration to the reactor. Peristaltic pumps P1 and P2 are computer controlled and produce modified flow rates between 9 and 91 mL/h with a cycle time of 5 min. However, at the reactor inlet the combined flow rate is always 100 mL/h and the concentrations of the substrates, G6P and GSSG, vary between 1 and 10 mM. The output signal produced is represented by the concentration profile of NADPH. To measure the concentration of NADPH, the stream leaving the reactor passes through a spectrophotometer and the optical density is measured continuously at 339 nm and recorded with the attached recorder.

In Figure 4.69 experimental results obtained when the basic system was operated in the packed bed reactor mode are presented. It can be seen that the experimental output signal obtained is a repetitive signal having a time period of 10 min. In this figure theoretical results are also presented. Simulations were carried out with various values of $K_{i,G6P}$ and considering five compartments in the reactor (i.e., the reactor behaves as a PFR). The immobilized enzymes were assumed to be distributed homogeneously in the reactor. Comparing the experimental and theoretical results, it can be seen that when inhibition of GR by G6P is considered, agreement improved between the theoretical and experimental results. Unlike previous cases in which the basic system was operated in a fed-batch reactor, here the theoretical results obtained when the value of $K_{i,G6P}$ used was the one determined experimentally (i.e., 8.4 mM) are quite close to the experimental results.

The interpretation of the experimental results presented in Figure 4.69 was extended to include inhibition of the enzyme G6PDH by NADPH with $K_{i,NADPH} = 0.027$ mM. A comparison between experimental and calculated results is shown in Figure 4.70. In this case better agreement is achieved when lower values of $K_{i,G6P}$ are employed, the values being in the range obtained in experiments carried out in a fed-batch reactor (0.15 to 1 mM).

When comparing experimental and theoretical results it should be mentioned that in addition to processes that are related to the reaction mechanisms but not considered in the model (see Section 4.3.6), several assumptions related to the operational mode are also made. For example, in the analytical model developed for the packed bed reactor it was assumed that no diffusion limitations are operative and that the immobilized enzymes are distributed in

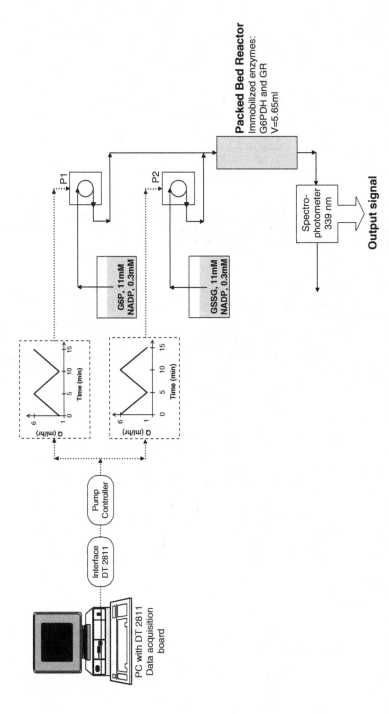

Figure 4.68 Configuration employed for operation of the basic system as a packed bed reactor. (……): control lines; (- - -): input information; (——): fluid flow lines; P1, P2, P3: peristaltic pumps; G6P: glucose-6-phosphate; GSSG: reduced glutathione.

113

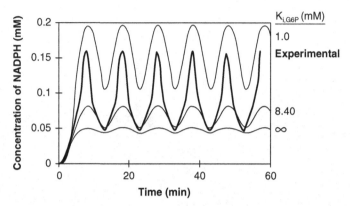

Figure 4.69 Experimental and theoretical results obtained for the basic system with G6PDH and GR when operated as a packed bed reactor. Theoretical results were obtained with $n = 5$ (i.e., assuming plug flow regimen), $V_{m,G6PDH} = 0.6$ mM/min and $V_{m,GR} = 0.7$ mM/min and considering G6P as an inhibitor of GR with the values of $K_{i,G6P}$ indicated.

the reactor homogeneously. This can lead to disagreement between the results obtained when different operation modes are employed. However, the analytical model can be used to predict the output signal with good accuracy, and this is very important in a complex system where this prediction is essential in the design process, in which determination of the operational parameters takes place.

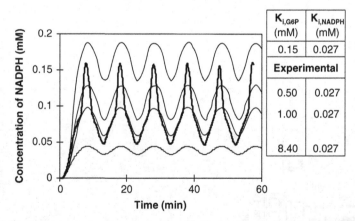

Figure 4.70 Experimental and theoretical results obtained for the basic system with G6PDH and GR when operated as a packed bed reactor. Theoretical results were obtained with $n = 5$ (i.e., assuming a plug flow regimen), $V_{m,G6PDH} = 0.6$ mM/min, and $V_{m,GR} = 0.7$ mM/min and considering G6P as an inhibitor of GR and NADPH as an inhibitor of G6PDH with the inhibition constant indicated above.

4.4 THE EXTENDED BASIC SYSTEM: THEORETICAL CONSIDERATIONS AND RESULTS

An extension of the basic system considered in this work is termed the extended basic system. This system was also designed to function as an information-processing unit and is characterized in Section 4.4.1. Its chracteristics as an information-processing unit are described in Section 4.4.2. In Section 4.4.3 the analytical model that was written for the extended basic system is presented. Using this model, numerical simulations were carried out and their results are presented in Section 4.4.4.

4.4.1 Characteristics of the Extended Basic System

The extended basic system shown in Figure 4.71 relies on the same reactions as those utilized in the basic system: reactions (1) and (2) of Section 4.1.1. In addition to the processes considered in the basic system, an external inhibitor for enzyme E_1 is fed into the system.

4.4.2 Extended Basic System as an Information-Processing Unit

The extended basic system is also designed to function as an information-processing unit with the same characteristics as those defined in Section 4.1.2 for the basic system. The difference between the systems arises from the composition of the input signal. In the extended basic system the input signal can follow one of the four options presented in Table 4.11. These options were chosen as representative of the experimental systems studied (see Section 4.5). The concentration profiles applied here are also defined

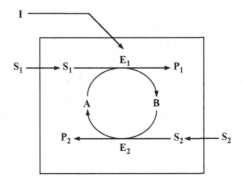

Figure 4.71 Extended basic system. S_1, S_2: substrates; P_1, P_2: products; E_1, E_2: participating enzymes; A,B: cofactors; I: external inhibitor to enzyme E_1.

Table 4.11   Input Signal in the Extended Basic System[a]

Option No.	$[I]_0$	$[S_1]_0$	$[S_2]_0$
1	—	$\bigwedge$	$\bigvee$
2	$\bigwedge$	—	—
3	$\bigwedge$	$\bigvee$	—
4	$\bigwedge$	—	$\bigvee$

[a]—: constant; $\bigwedge$, $\bigvee$: variable, following the profiles described in Section 4.1.2 and Figure 4.2.

with the parameters detailed in Section 4.1.2: cycle time (τ), period time (π), range, and amplitude.

4.4.3   Analytical Model for the Extended Basic System

The analytical models developed in this part are based on those written for the basic system and presented in Section 4.1.3. The extended basic system is considered useful for information processing only with continuous operational modes. This is due to the fact that the inhibitor is not consumed in the reactor, and in a fed-batch reactor it accumulates and causes only decay effects. Therefore, the analytical model presented here refers only to a continuous reactor.

Applying the compartmental analysis approach leads to equations (32) to (37), which hold for both the basic and the extended basic systems. When the latter is considered, the following equation should also be used:

$$\frac{d\,[I]_i}{dt} = \frac{Q}{V_i}\left([I]_{i-1} - [I]_i\right) \tag{72}$$

Equations (32) to (37) are related to the reaction mechanism considered. For the extended basic system, the inhibition process is taken into account in rate equations r_1 and r_2. The options considered in this study are detailed in the Sections 4.4.3a and b.

Initial conditions for equations (32) to (37) and (72) are defined by the concentrations of the substrates, products, enzymes, and external inhibitor in the reactor compartments at the onset of operation (at time $t = 0$); for $1 \le i \le n$,

$$\begin{aligned} [S_1]_i &= 0, & [S_2]_i &= 0 \\ [P_1]_i &= 0, & [P_2]_i &= 0 \\ [A]_i &= 0, & [B]_i &= 0 \\ [I]_i &= 0 \end{aligned} \tag{73}$$

As indicated in Figure 4.71, the feed stream to the reactor is composed of the substrates S_1 and S_2, the cofactor A, and the external inhibitor. Thus, for any time t, the following equation holds:

$$
\begin{array}{ll}
[S_1]_0 = f_1(t), & [S_2]_0 = f_2(t) \\
[P_1]_0 = 0, & [P_2]_0 = 0 \\
[A]_0 = f_3(t), & [B]_0 = 0 \\
[I]_0 = f_4(t) &
\end{array}
\tag{74}
$$

The set of equations (32) to (37), (49), and (74) are solved numerically according to the Runge–Kutta method [145] with initial conditions as defined in equation (73).

a. Ping-Pong Mechanism and External Inhibition   In this case the external compound fed into the system is considered a "dead-end" inhibitor to the enzyme E_1. Such an inhibitor reacts with one or more enzyme forms to yield a complex that cannot participate in the reaction. When the ping-pong mechanism is considered and the inhibitor combines with the enzyme form that reacts with S_1 (i.e., I is competitive with respect to S_1), the rate equation r_1 becomes [146]

$$
r_{1,i} = \frac{V_{m,1}[S_1]_i[A]_i}{\{1 + [I]_i/K_I\} K_{m,S_1}[A]_i + K_{m,A}[S_1]_i + [S_1]_i[A]_i}
\tag{75}
$$

b. Ping-Pong Mechanism, Product Inhibition, and External Inhibition   In this case the processes described in Sections 4.1.3.2c and 4.4.3a take place simultaneously in reaction (1). For this case, the rate equation for reaction (1) becomes [146]

$$
r_{1,i} = \frac{V_{m,1}[S_1]_i[A]_i}{\{1 + [I]_i/K_I\} K_{m,S_1}[A]_i + \{1 + [B]_i/K_{i,B}\} K_{m,A}[S_1]_i + [S_1]_i[A]_i}
\tag{76}
$$

4.4.4   Results of Numerical Simulations for the Extended Basic System

In this section, results of numerical simulations are presented for the case when the extended basic system is operated in a continuous reactor. Here, the inhibitor enters the reactor as a component of the feed stream and affects the enzyme E_1 (it is competitive with S_1). In Figures 4.72 to 4.77 the effects of the system parameters on the concentration of B in a PFR with an external inhibitor are presented. The sets of the basic values used for the parameters involved are given in Table 4.12, set I.

Table 4.12 Numerical Values of the Operational Parameters Used in Simulations of the Extended Basic System When Operated as a Packed Bed Reactor

Parameter	Symbol	Units	Set I	Set II
Volume of the reactor	V	mL	6	5.65
Volumetric flow rate	Q	mL/h	100	100
Cycle time	τ	min	5	5
Concentration range of S_1 in the feed stream	$S_{1,0}$	mM	1	5
Concentration range of S_2 in the feed stream	$S_{2,0}$	mM	1	5
Concentration range of the external inhibitor in the feed stream	I_0	mM	1–10	ind.[a]
Concentration of A in the feed stream	A_0	mM	0.3	0.3
Michaelis constant for S_1	K_{m,S_1}	mM	0.156	0.156
Michaelis constant for S_2	K_{m,S_2}	mM	0.0469	0.0469
Michaelis constant for A	$K_{m,A}$	mM	0.076	0.076
Michaelis constant for B	$K_{m,B}$	mM	0.0266	0.0266
Inhibition constant for the external inhibitor	K_I	mM	ind.[a]	1
Maximal rate of the reaction $S_1 + A \rightarrow P_1 + B$	$V_{m,1}$	mM/min	0.5	0.5
Maximal rate of the reaction $S_2 + B \rightarrow P_2 + A$	$V_{m,2}$	mM/min	0.5	0.5

ind.: indicated in the figure.

Figure 4.72 presents the effect of the inhibition constant K_I. In this case the substrates are fed at constant concentrations, and the concentration of the external inhibitor in the feed stream changes according to the function described in Section 4.1.2. It can be seen that an oscillatory signal is obtained and its amplitude increases as K_I increases from 0.001 mM to 0.1 mM. Another increase in the value of K_I from 0.1 mM to 1 mM causes the opposite effect, and the amplitude decreases drastically. This relationship between the amplitude of the output signal and the value of K_I is presented in Figure 4.73, where a bell-shaped curve is observed. The amplitude of the input signal is 9 mM; therefore, the system presented decreases this amplitude by 600 or more. This enables one to obtain very fine amplitudes that cannot be obtained by means of flow rates.

Figure 4.74 presents the effect of constant substrate concentration in the feed stream on the concentration profile of B. It can be seen that the amplitude of the oscillatory output signal obtained increases when $[S_1]_0$ and $[S_2]_0$ increase from 0.1 mM to 10 mM. Another increase in $[S_1]_0$ and $[S_2]_0$

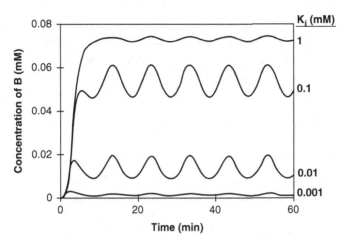

Figure 4.72   Effect of K_I on the concentration profile of B in the extended basic system when operated as a PFR ($n = 5$). The values of K_I are indicated above, $[S_1]_0 = [S_2]_{,0} = 46.6$ mM, and the values used for all other parameters are given in Table 4.12, set I.

causes a decrease in the the amplitude of the output signal. This relationship between the amplitude of the output signal and the values of $[S_1]_0$ and $[S_2]_0$ is presented in Figure 4.75. The effect obtained here resembles the one obtained in Figures 4.72 and 4.73, where K_I was the variable parameter. When this system is operated practically, changes in K_I are achieved by changing the external inhibitor, but changes in $[S_1]_0$ and $[S_2]_0$ are achieved more easily by changing these concentrations in the feed stream.

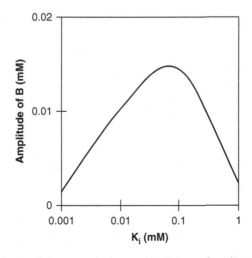

Figure 4.73   Amplitude of the concentration profile of B as a function of K_I. Data are taken from Figure 4.72.

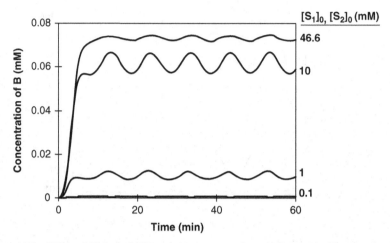

Figure 4.74   Effect of $[S_1]_0$ and $[S_2]_0$ on the concentration profile of B in the extended basic system when operated as a PFR ($n = 5$). The values of $[S_1]_0$ and $[S_2]_0$ are indicated above, $K_1 = 1$ mM, and the values used for all other parameters are given in Table 4.12, set I.

Figure 4.76 presents the effect of the flow rate on the output signal obtained. It can be seen that an increase in the flow rate through the reactor leads to an increase in the amplitude of the oscillatory output signal obtained. This increase in the flow rate also causes a phase shift in the output signal, which is presented in Figure 4.77. It can be seen that large phase shifts are obtained when low flow rates are employed, and these tend to reach a constant value when high flow rates are employed.

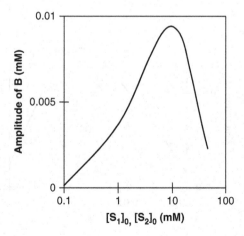

Figure 4.75   Amplitude of the concentration profile B as a function of $[S_1]_0$ and $[S_2]_0$. Data are taken from Figure 4.74.

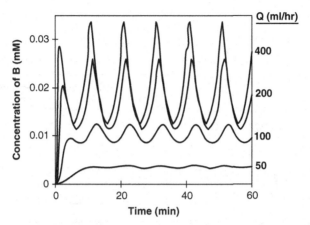

Figure 4.76   Effect of flow rate on the concentration profile of B in the extended basic system when operated as a PFR ($n = 5$). The values of Q are indicated, $K_I = 1$ mM, and the values used for all other parameters are given in Table 4.12, set I.

The calculations discussed above (Figures 4.72 to 4.77) were performed for a PFR. Figures 4.78 to 4.80 refer to a packed bed reactor with $n = 3$. In this case the effect of the concentration range of the external inhibitor on the signal obtained was investigated. The data in Figures 4.78 to 4.80 differ from one another with respect to the cycle time, τ, of the concentration profile of

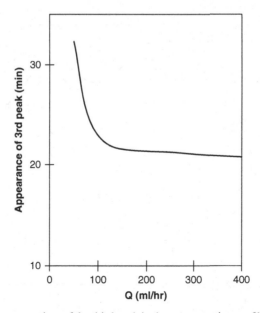

Figure 4.77   Appearance time of the third peak in the concentration profile of B as a function of Q. Data are taken from Figure 4.76.

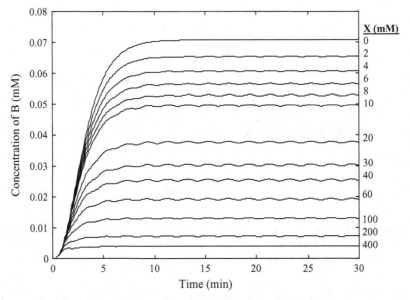

Figure 4.78   Effect of an external inhibitor on the concentration profile of B in the extended basic system when operated as a packed bed reactor ($n = 3$). The external inhibitor concentration varies between 0 and X. The values of X are indicated above, the cycle time (τ) is 1 min, and the values used for all other parameters are given in Table 4.12, set II.

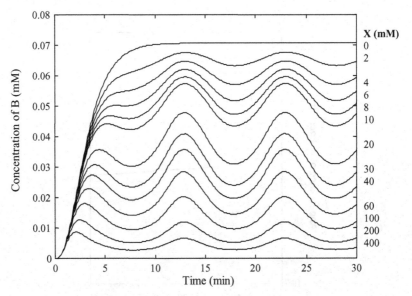

Figure 4.79   Effect of an external inhibitor on the concentration profile of B in the extended basic system when operated as a packed bed reactor ($n = 3$). The external inhibitor concentration varies between 0 and X. The values of X are indicated above, the cycle time (τ) is 5 min, and the values used for all other parameters are given in Table 4.12, set II.

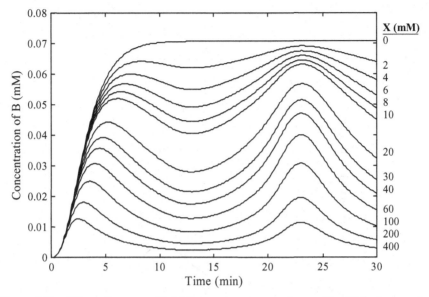

Figure 4.80 Effect of an external inhibitor on the concentration profile of B in the extended basic system when operated as a packed bed reactor ($n = 3$). The external inhibitor concentration varies between 0 and X. The values of X are indicated above, the cycle time (τ) is 10 min, and the values used for all other parameters are given in Table 4.12, set II.

the external inhibitor in the feed stream. It can be seen that in the three cases presented ($\tau = 1, 5$, and 10 min), an increase in the concentration range of the input signal first causes an increase in the amplitude of the oscillatory signal obtained. This amplitude reaches a maximal value, and then an additional increase in the concentration range of the input signal causes a decrease in this amplitude.

The signals obtained with different values of τ are compared in Figure 4.81. In all the cases presented here the concentration of the inhibitor in the feed stream varies between 0 and 20 mM, and it can be seen that an increase in the cycle time leads to an increase in the amplitude and a decrease in the time period of the oscillatory signals obtained.

For the case presented in Figures 4.78 to 4.80 a close system can be designed. The purpose of this system is to reach the maximal possible amplitude for the output signal using a feedback algorithm. Thus, the process is based on measurement of the amplitude obtained for the output signal, comparing this amplitude to the former one and then calculating the gradient of the function described in Figure 4.81. Using this gradient the concentration of the external inhibitor in the feed stream is corrected. This process is repeated until the gradient obtained is close enough to zero.

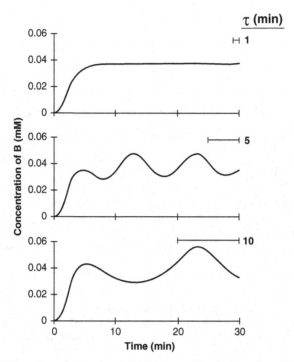

Figure 4.81 Effect of τ of an external inhibitor on the concentration profile of B in the extended basic system when operated as a packed bed reactor ($n = 3$). The external inhibitor concentration varies between 0 and 20 mM. Data for $\tau = 1$, 5, and 10 min are taken from Figures 4.78, 4.79, and 4.80, respectively. The size of the bars indicates the values of τ.

5

DISCUSSION

5.1 THE BASIC SYSTEM

The ability of the basic system to perform information-processing functions was examined using a series of analytical models developed in this study. These models are also designed to serve as a tool for directing the experiments in which the basic system is operated. In this respect the input signals were related to those used in the experimental part.

The basic system was operated as a fed-batch reactor and as a continuous reactor. The fed batch was used as a first implementation due to its simplicity of operation. However, in such a reactor dilution takes place during operation and therefore the operation conditions should involve a low flow rate and high volume of reaction mixture. Also, this mode of operation requires sizable amounts of the soluble enzymes, and the total operation time is limited.

When immobilized enzymes are employed in a continuous reactor, many of these limitations are avoided. Moreover, in this case the output signal is recorded at the reactor outlet, and this procedure therefore cannot affect the processes taking place in the reactor, and the signals obtained can be used in another system as actual concentrations without conversion. Yet, in this configuration the cofactor enters the reactor in the feed stream, which requires large amounts of cofactor, especially when a high flow rate is employed.

Information Processing by Biochemical Systems: Neural Network–Type Configurations, By Orna Filo and Noah Lotan
Copyright © 2010 John Wiley & Sons, Inc.

5.1.1 Fed-Batch Reactor: Numerical Simulations

The main information-processing function obtained when the basic system is operated as a fed batch reactor is conversion of the continuous input signal to signals characterized by "ON" (nonzero concentration) and "OFF" (zero concentration) periods, when each period lasts for the entire cycle time of the input signal. The numerical simulation results show that the output signals produced by the basic system depend to a large extent on the reaction mechanism and the inhibition processes involved as well as on the values of $V_{m,i}$, $K_{m,j}$, and $S_{i,0}$ ($i = 1, 2$) and the relationships between them. From these results some empirical rules could be derived. Thus, it was concluded that in order to obtain ON/OFF output signals, the following conditions should be fulfilled:

- The values of $V_{m,i}$ (in mM/min) should be around 20 times greater than the highest value of $K_{m,j}$ (in mM).
- The average values of $S_{i,0}$ should be about 10^3 times larger than the highest value of $K_{m,j}$.

5.1.2 Continuous Reactor: Numerical Simulations

When the basic system was operated as a continuous packed bed reactor, the analytical model developed here allows us to describe the performance of all types of reactors, from a continuous stirred tank reactor (CSTR) to a plug flow reactor (PFR). It was shown that the information-processing function depends on the reactor type, the flow rate through the reactor, the concentration of the cofactor in the feed stream, the values of $V_{m,i}$, the presence of internal inhibitors, and the cycle time of the input signal.

The information-processing function carried out in continuous reactors produces the following signals:

- ON/OFF signals (periods of 20/20, 10/30, or 30/10 min for an input signal with a cycle time of 20 min).
- Repetitive oscillatory signals with different amplitudes, different phases, and time periods similar to those of the input signals.

5.1.3 Assessment of Experimental Results

The basic system was implemented experimentally utilizing the enzymes G6PDH and GR in a fed-batch reactor (soluble enzymes) and a packed bed reactor (immobilized enzymes). The most important conclusions of these experiments are that cyclic enzyme systems:

* Can actually perform information-processing functions.
* Can produce the signal types predicted by the analytical model.
* Require that for accurate prediction of their function, one must be familiar with all the processes that take place in the system (e.g., inhibition processes).

It should be pointed out that this is the first time that such characteristics have been found and reported.

5.2   THE EXTENDED BASIC SYSTEM

This new system is an extension of the basic system discussed above. In the extended basic system an external inhibitor is also involved in the processes taking place. This component provides an additional path for control of the enzymic activity. Thus, whereas in the basic system the input signal is composed of concentration profiles of the consumable substrates, here the input signal contains a component that is an effector for one of the enzymes but is not consumed in the reactions. Due to this characteristic, this system is considered useful in terms of information processing only with continuous operational modes.

For the extended basic system the output signals obtained were repetitive oscillatory signals, with a time period similar to that of the input signal but with different amplitudes and phases. It was shown that this amplitude is related to the system parameters. Therefore, the input signal characteristics can be chosen according to the amplitude required for the output signal. The extended basic system was implemented experimentally in a packed bed reactor utilizing the same enzymes as those used for the basic system (i.e., G6PDH and GR). The results obtained show that the extended basic system produces the signal types predicted by the analytical model and can actually perform information-processing functions.

5.3   BIOCHEMICAL NETWORKS

The representation of nerve cells as symbolic devices such as perceptrons led to the development of the computer-based models termed artificial neural networks. Since proteins in general, and enzymes in particular, are capable of accepting inputs and producing outputs, it seems inescapable to conclude that the interconnected network of enzyme-based reactions will share some of the properties of artificial neural networks and to a large extent will resemble natural information-processing systems.

A series of networks were considered in this study. In all cases the networks were built of a number of basic systems (biochemical neurons), and communication between the individual neurons was achieved by chemical species passing from one neuron to another, where they participate in processes taking place therein. This type of communication is operative in natural neuronic systems, where "information" from one neuron to the other is passed as neurotransmitter molecules crossing the synapses connecting the participating neurons.

The networks considered in this study are of three main types (identified as A, B, and C), differing from one another by the mode of connection between the participating biochemical neurons (see Table 5.1). For each network considered, an analytical model was written describing the performance of the network in kinetic terms. As the first stage in this program, analytical models were developed for the case when the reactions of the biochemical networks take place in fed-batch reactors. It is envisaged that these models will be extended to packed bed reactors in the future.

In this part the main interest was to examine the information-processing abilities of the networks and to assess the advantage of a network over a single basic system. The main information-processing functions achieved by the network systems studied are indicated in Table 5.1. It can be seen that both single neurons and networks can perform basic switching operations. However, unlike a single neuron, the networks can also perform more complex processes (i.e., division and pacemaking). Moreover, any performance of the networks is dependent on the network type (i.e., A, B, or C), on the number

Table 5.1 Characteristics and Information-Processing Operations of Biochemical Networks

Network	Type	Number of Basic Systems	Number of Substrates in the Input	Number of Outputs	Information-Processing Operations
A	Fully connected	n	$2n$	$4n + 2$	Switching Division by 2
B	Feedforward	n	2	$4n + 2$	Switching Division by 2 Pacemaker
C	Fully connected	n	2	$2n + 4$	Switching Division by 2 Division by 4

of basic systems connected in the network, and on the internal parameters of the biochemical reactions (e.g., $K_{m,j}$ and $V_{m,i}$).

5.4 COMPARING ARTIFICIAL NEURAL NETWORKS WITH BIOCHEMICAL NETWORKS

To learn the characteristic properties of the biochemical systems considered in this study and to assess their ability to perform as ANNs, a direct comparison between the two is made here. In so doing it should be noted that there is no universally accepted definition of an artificial neural network. Therefore, we refer here to the characteristics of ANNs summarized from some of the definitions available in the literature [17–22]. The next step is to examine if the characteristics mentioned above can also be found in the biochemical networks proposed in this study. These characteristics are compared one by one in Table 5.2.

5.5 COMPARING BIOCHEMICAL NETWORKS TO COMPUTATIONAL MODELS

In 1936, A.M. Turing defined a class of abstract machines now called *Turing machines* [150,151]. A Turing machine is a finite-state machine associated with a special type of environment: its tape, in which it can store (and later recover) sequences of symbols. At each moment the machine gets its input stimulus by reading the symbol written at a certain point along the tape. The response of the machine may change that symbol and also move the machine a small distance either way along the tape. The result is that the stimulus for the next cycle of operation will come from a different "square" of the tape, and the machine may thus read a symbol that was written there long ago. This means that the machine has access to a rudimentary exterior memory in addition to that provided within its finite-state part. Since no limit is placed on the amount of tape available, this memory has, in effect, an infinite capacity. Turing discovered that he could set up these machines to make very complex computations [150,151].

Despite its simplicity, the Turing machine models the computing capability of a general-purpose computer, and since 1936 it has been the standard accepted model of universal computation. The proposition, often called the *Church–Turing thesis*, says that any process which could naturally be called an effective procedure can be realized by a Turing machine. In other words, this thesis states that no realizable computing device can be more powerful than a Turing machine [150,151]. It is, however, of interest to discuss the

Table 5.2   Comparison Between Artificial Neural Networks and Biochemical Networks

ANNs	Biochemical Networks
1. ANNs are combination of rules (software) and hardware.	The entire biochemical network can be seen as the hardware component and does not need attached software in order to function.
2. The network is built of a number of elementary processing elements (neurons or nodes).	The biochemical network is built of a number of processing elements (i.e., the biochemical neurons). These are the enzymic basic systems. The term *elementary* is not an absolute one. However, the processing based on a few enzymic reactions is less complex than the processing of electrical signals as achieved by natural nerve cells.
3. The neurons are highly interconnected and information is transferred from one element to another along the connecting lines.	The enzymic basic systems can be highly interconnected, due to chemical components that participate in processes that take place in more than one biochemical neuron.
4. The neurons operate in parallel.	When all the components that are required by the enzymic reactions in the network are present in the reaction medium, all the enzymes operate in parallel. Moreover, each enzyme recognizes its specific substrates only.
5. The network responds to external inputs by producing well-defined outputs.	For an enzymic system, the input is the concentration profiles of chemical species fed into the system, while the output is the concentration profiles of all chemical species involved in the system. Under given conditions, the relationship between input and output is uniquely defined by the reaction mechanism and the pertinent rate equations.
6. Each neuron in the network operates only on local information.	In the biochemical network each biochemical neuron works only with the substrates required for the specific reactions involved and is not affected by the reactions that take place in other neurons, unless they share a particular component.
7. The network stores information as the synaptic weights and makes them available for further use.	In the biochemical network, the basic information is the kinetic mechanism and the kinetic parameters of the participating enzymes, and this was stored during evolutionary processes. This information is used when reactions are carried out. Therefore, in biochemical networks, information is not stored in the connection strengths but in the enzymes catalyzing the reactions.

Table 5.2   *(Continued)*

ANNs	Biochemical Networks
8. The network function is determined by the network structure (i.e., the particular mode by which the individual neurons are connected to one another), the connection strengths (synaptic weights) (i.e., the quantitative rules defining the information transfer), and the processing performed at the individual neuron.	In this study we showed that the biochemical networks function according to the mode of connection between the basic systems (e.g., network A, B, or C), and also according to the processing performed at each neuron (i.e., reaction mechanism or kinetic constants). For the biochemical systems, the strengths of connection between basic elements (i.e., synaptic weights) is represented by the concentration of the component that is shared between the neurons.
9. The networks can "adapt" themselves to produce a desired output. This adaptation is usually achieved by changing the synaptic weights, and this process is defined as "learning." Some networks carry out the learning process by relying on task examples.	In the biochemical network, the processing elements do not learn from task examples, but the knowledge is already "built in." For example, an enzyme recognizes a specific substrate and applies a specific rate for the catalytic reaction, as a function of the particular conditions, pH, temperature, and so on. Therefore, in such systems, adaptation is implemented by adjusting the catalytic characteristics according to environmental conditions and following laws already "built in" by evolution.

computing capabilities of the biochemical networks proposed in this study and to examine whether their special characteristics enable them to perform as Turing machines or as different machines, even more powerful than those conceived based on the Turing model.

Neural networks are usually studied in association with their applications in the areas of vision, speech processing, robotics, signal processing, and many other fields. However, it is of great interest to examine the computational power and computational capabilities of these systems. An attempt to explain the computational basis of neural networks is presented in the work of Siegelmann and colleagues [152–155]. In these studies particular interest is given to recurrent neural network models. These networks have no concept of "layers," and they allow for loops and cycles that give rise to a dynamical system. Recurrent neural networks are able to incorporate memory and, due to this characteristic, can provide a computational model. A feedforward network supports no memory and therefore cannot provide a computational model. The computational models discussed by Siegelmann and co-workers

[152–155] consider continuous recurrent networks with a finite number of neurons in which the activation function σ is the saturated-linear function:

$$\sigma(x) := \begin{cases} 0 & \text{if } x < 0 \\ x & \text{if } 0 \leq x \leq 1 \\ 1 & \text{if } x > 1 \end{cases}$$

The networks are also specified by sets of coefficients called *weights* and by a subset of p output processors that are used to communicate the outputs of the network to the environment. These studies consider a uniform model in which the structure of the networks and the values of the weights do not change in time. The outputs of each processor are the only parameters that change with time. Siegelmann et al. [152–155] show that the computational power of these uniform recurrent networks depends on the classes of numbers utilized as weights:

- If the weights are integers, the neurons may assume binary activation values only and the network accepts a regular language [155].
- If the weights are rational numbers, the network is equivalent in power to the Turing machine model [152–155].
- When weights are general real numbers, the network turns out to have super-Turing capabilities [152–155].

Now we can look at the biochemical networks developed in this work and compare them to the recurrent networks discussed above. Network A (Section 4.2.1) and Network C (Section 4.2.3) are fully connected to one another, and the information flows back and forth from each neuron to all the others. This situation is very much like the one described for recurrent neural networks, and in these cases, memory, which is a necessary to demonstrate computational power, is clearly incorporated in the networks. Network B (Section 4.2.2) is a feedforward network and thus appears to have no memory in this form. However, when we examine the processes taking place in the biochemical neuron more carefully, we can see that the enzymic reactions take into account the concentration of the relevant substrates present in the system. These substrates can be fed as inputs at any time t. However, part of them also remained from the reactions that took place at time $t - 1$, and thus the enzymic system in every form is influenced by the processes that took place at early stages. Hence, memory is always incorporated.

The activation function of the biochemical neuron is defined by the reaction mechanism and the pertinent rate equations. This function is actually a set of differential equations derived from mass balances for the components taking part in the enzymic reactions in each biochemical neuron (see Section 4.1.3).

This activation function is much more complicated then the saturated linear function used in recurrent neural networks [152–155] and is actually established by the biochemical system. According to Siegelmann [154], use of a complicated activation function does not increase the computational power of the network.

The recurrent network models assume that the structure of the network, as well as the values of the weights, do not change in time. Moreover, only the activation values (i.e., the output of each processor that is used in the next iteration) changes in time. In the biochemical network one cannot separate outputs and weights. The outputs of one biochemical neurons are time dependent and enter the following biochemical neurons as they are. However, the coefficients involved in these biochemical processes are the kinetic constants that appear in the rate equations, and these constants are real numbers. The inputs considered in biochemical networks are continuous analog numbers that change over time. The inputs to the recurrent neural networks are sets of binary numbers.

There are many similarities between recurrent neural networks and the biochemical networks presented in this work. However, the dissimilarities reviewed here are very closely related to the inherent characteristics of biochemical systems, such as their kinetic equations. Thus, in future work one may consider recurrent neural networks that are similar to biochemical networks— having the same activation function and the same connections between neurons—and this approach will allow one to assess their computational capabilities.

In another study, Kilian and Siegelmann [156] introduced a new type of automaton called the *alarm clock machine*. In this study, alarm clocks are replaced by dynamic counters, which are very much like the input signals that are introduced into biochemical networks (see Figure 4.2). They showed that alarm clock machines are Turing universal and that they can be implemented by a sigmoidal recurrent neural network. Although our biochemical networks can also produce the types of signals used as dynamic counters, these signals can be produced simply in other ways, such as they were produced for the input signal in this work. Thus, in this context the use of biochemical networks is not advantageous.

Other types of "machines" that are not based on neural networks were also suggested as continuous-time models. Pour-El [157] constructed a general-purpose analog computer using a finite number of the following units:

- Integrator
- Constant multiplier
- Adder
- Variable multiplier
- Constant function

According to this model, it is required that two inputs and two outputs never be interconnected, and in addition, each input is connected to at most one output.

Another model for an analog computer was suggested by Rubel [158,159]. Called an *extended analog computer*, it is also based on a finite number of functions that are applied on independent variables. The machine consists of several levels, and the outputs of level $N - 1$ are used as the inputs of level N. The computing is achieved by "black boxes" of various kinds, such as adders, multipliers, substituters, and differentiators.

To build a machine based on the models suggested by Pour-El and Rubel [157–159] and on the biochemical units developed in this work, the biochemical units should be able to perform the mathematical operations defined above. In this work it was shown that networks A, B, and C can act as constant multipliers (see Table 5.1). Other units will have to be defined in the future.

6

CONCLUSIONS

This study brings us to the following main conclusions:

1. Enzyme-based biochemical neurons can be built, analyzed, and operated using some of the basic principles of neural networks.
2. Enzyme-based biochemical networks can be designed and analyzed using basic principles of enzyme kinetics and compartmental analysis procedures.
3. This study reveals many similarities between biochemical networks and artificial neural networks. Yet there are also major differences between ANNs and biochemical networks, and these address particularly the principles on which the learning process is achieved. Thus, in most ANNs the strength of connections is modified by presenting the network with a "teaching" input and applying a learning algorithm, whereas in biochemical networks such a process does not take place. In the latter, for a given set of operational conditions, the performance of the network is predictable since all the knowledge is already "built in" within the enzymes. This knowledge was acquired during evolutionary processes or was provided artificially by chemical or genetic modifications.
4. In biochemical networks, adaptation takes place by responding to changes in environmental conditions, and this is achieved by adjusting the kinetic parameters. This adjustment leads to changes in the

Information Processing by Biochemical Systems: Neural Network–Type Configurations, By Orna Filo and Noah Lotan
Copyright © 2010 John Wiley & Sons, Inc.

concentrations of the chemical species transferred from one neuron to another. As these species provide the connection between individual neurons, a change in their concentration is equivalent to a change in the synaptic weights.

The concepts of ANNs were inspired by studies of biological systems. Thus, biochemical networks such as those studied here are closer to biological systems for information processing than are the ANNs. This is because the biological networks and the biochemical systems for information processing use the same "language" and the same hardware (the biological molecules). As such, the biochemical networks provide unique advantages, and these should be utilized in the service of further progress.

REFERENCES

1. T. Kaminuma and G. Matsumoto, Eds., *Biocomputers: The Next Generation from Japan*, Chapman & Hall, London, 1991.

2. D. Bray, Intracellular signalling as a parallel distributed process, *J. Theor. Biol.*, **143**, 215–231 (1990).

3. M. H. Capstick, W. P. L. Marnane, and R. Pethig, Biologic computational building blocks, *Computer*, **25**(11), 22–29 (1992).

4. D. Bray, R. B. Bourret, and M. I. Simon, Computer simulation of the phosphorylation cascade controlling bacterial chemotaxis, *Mol. Biol. Cell*, **4**, 469–482 (1993).

5. R. C. Paton, Some computational models at the cellular level, *BioSystems*, **29**, 63–75 (1993).

6. M. Conrad, Scaling of efficiency in programmable and non-programmable systems, *BioSystems*, **35**, 161–166 (1995).

7. P. C. Marijuan, Enzymes, artificial cells and the nature of biological information, *BioSystems*, **35**, 167–170 (1995).

8. M. Conrad, Cross scale interactions in biomolecular information processing, *BioSystems*, **35**, 157–160 (1995).

9. R. Rosen, Two factor models, neural nets, and biochemical automata, *J. Theor. Biol.*, **15**, 282–297 (1967).

10. R. Rosen, Recent development in the theory of control and regulation of cellular processes, *Int. Rev. Cytol.*, **23**, 25–88 (1968).

11. R. R. Kampfner and M. Conrad, Computational modeling of evolutionary learning processes in the brain, *Bull. Math. Biol.*, **45**, 931–968 (1983).

12. R. R. Kampfner and M. Conrad, Sequential behaviour and stability properties of enzymatic neuron networks, *Bull. Math. Biol.*, **46**, 969–980 (1983).

13. K. G. Kirby and M. Conrad, The enzymatic neuron as a reaction-diffusion network of cyclic nucleotides, *Bull. Math. Biol.*, **46**, 765–783 (1984).

14. S. Neuschl and P. Menhart, Networks based on enzyme type neurons, in *Molecular Electronics: Science and Technology*, A. Aviram and A. Bross, Eds., Engineering Foundation, New York, 1989, pp. 167–173.

15. R. P. Lippmann, An introduction to computing with neural nets, *IEEE ASSP Mag.*, **4**, 4–22 (1987).

16. W. T. Katz, J. W. Snell, and M. B. Merickel, Artificial neural networks, in *Methods in Enzymology*, Vol. **210**, L. Brand and M. J. Johnson, Eds., Academic Press, New York, 1992, pp. 610–636.

17. M. Caudill, Neural networks primer, Part I, *AI Expert*, Dec. 1987, pp. 46–52.

18. *DARPA Neural Network Study*, AFCEA International Press, Fairfax, VA, 1988.

19. I. Aleksander and H. Morton, *An Introduction to Neural Computing*, Chapman & Hall, London, 1990.

20. J. M. Zurada, *Introduction to Artificial Neural Systems*, PWS Publishing, Boston, 1992.

21. A. Nigrin, *Neural Networks for Pattern Recognition*, MIT Press, Cambridge, MA, 1993.

22. S. Haykin, *Neural Networks: A Comprehensive Foundation*, Macmillan, New York, 1994.

23. W. S. McCulloch and W. Pitts, A logical calculus of the ideas imminent in nervous activity, *Bull. Math. Biophys.*, **5**, 115–133 (1943).

24. D. O. Hebb, *The Organization of Behavior*, Wiley, New York, 1949.

25. F. T. Hong, Molecular electronics: science and technology for the future, *IEEE Eng. Med. Biol.*, **13**(1), 25–32 (1994).

26. M. Conrad, Molecular computing paradigms, *Computer*, **11**, 6–9 (1992).

27. R. W. Munn, Molecules as electronic components? *BioSystems*, **27**, 207–211 (1992).

28. R. R. Birge, D. S. K. Govender, R. B. Gross, A. F. Lawrence, J. A. Stuart, J. R. Tallent, E. Tan, and B. W. Vought, Bioelectronics, three-dimensional memories and hybrid computers, *International Electron Devices Meeting 1994, Technical Digest*, pp. 3–6.

29. A. Chiabrera, E. D. Zitti, F. Costa, and G. M. Bisio, Physical limits of integration and information processing in molecular systems, *J. Phys. D*, **22**, 1571–1579 (1989).

30. A. Aviram, Molecules for memory, logic, and amplification, *J. Am. Chem. Soc.*, **110**, 5687–5692 (1988).

31. A. Aviram, Molecular Electronics-Science and Technology, *Angew. Chem. Int. Ed. Engl.*, **28**, 520–521 (1989).

32. F. L. Carter, Electron tunneling in short periodic arrays, in *Molecular Electronic Devices*, F. L. Carter, Ed., Marcel Dekker, New York, 1982, pp. 121–136.

33. R. M. Metzger and C. A. Panetta, Toward organic rectifiers, in *Molecular Electronic Devices II*, F. L. Carter, Ed., Marcel Dekker, New York, 1987, pp. 5–26.

34. R. M. Metzger and C. A. Panetta, Langmuir–Blodgett films of potential organic rectifiers, in *Molecular Electronics: Science and Technology*, A. Aviram and A. Bross, Eds., Engineering Foundation, New York 1989, pp. 293–300.

35. A. Parasanna de Silva and K. R. A. S. Sandanayake, Fluoresence "Off–On" signaling upon linear recognition and binding of α,ω-alkanediyldiammonium ions by 9,10-bis{(1-aza-4,7,10,13,16-pentaoxacyclooctadecyl)methyl}anthracene, *Angew. Chem. Int. Ed. Engl.*, **29**(10), 1173–1175 (1990).

36. S. Nespurek, Molecular optical memories and switches based on photochromic dihydropyridines, *BioSystems*, **27**, 213–218 (1992).

37. A. Parasanna de Silva, H. Q. N. Gunaratne, and C. P. McCoy, A molecular photonic AND gate based on fluorescent signalling, *Nature*, **364**, 42–44 (1993).

38. S. Nespurek and J. Sworakowski, Electroactive and photochromic molecular materials for wires, switches and memories, *IEEE Eng. Med. Biol.*, **13**(1), 45–57 (1994).

39. D. Gust, T. A. Moore, and L. Moore, Photosynthesis mimics as molecular electronic devices, *IEEE Eng. Med. Biol.*, **13**(1), 58–66 (1994).

40. H. Kuhn, Organized monolayer assemblies, *IEEE Eng. Med. Biol.*, **13**(1), 33–44 (1994).

41. C. Nicolini, From neural network to biomolecular electronics, ICANN '94. Proceedings of the International Conference on Artificial Neural Networks, Vol. 2, pp. 1477–1482.

42. R. S. Phadke, Immobilization of enzymes/coenzymes for molecular electronics applications, *BioSystems*, **35**, 179–182 (1995).

43. M. Aizawa, Molecular interfacing for protein molecular devices and neurodevices, *IEEE Eng. Med. Biol.*, **13**(1), 94–102 (1994).

44. N. Lotan, G. Ashkenazi, S. Tuchman, S. Nehamkin, and S. Sideman, Molecular bioelectronics biomaterials, *Mol. Cryst. Liq. Cryst.*, **236**, 95–104 (1993).

45. N. G. Rambidi, V. M. Zamalin, and Y. M. Sandler, Molecular information processing devices and artificial intelligence problems, *J. Mol. Electron.*, **4**, S39–S48 (1988).

46. N. G. Rambidi, On design principles for functionally flexible molecular devices, in *Molecular Electronics: Science and Technology*, A. Aviram and A. Bross, Eds., Engineering Foundation, New York, 1989, pp. 205–211.

47. N. G. Rambidi, D. S. Chernavskii, and Y. M. Sandler, Towards a biomolecular computer: 1. Ways, means, objectives, *J. Mol. Electron.*, **7**, 105–114 (1991).

48. N. G. Rambidi and D. S. Chernavskii, Towards a biomolecular computer: 2. Information processing and computing devices based on biochemical non-linear dynamic systems, *J. Mol. Electron.*, **7**, 115–125 (1991).

49. N. G. Rambidi, Non-discrete biomolecular computing, *Computer*, **11**, 51–54 (1992).

50. N. G. Rambidi, Towards a biomolecular computer, *BioSystems*, **27**, 219–222 (1992).

51. N. G. Rambidi, Non-discrete biomolecular computing: an approach to computational complexity, *BioSystems*, **31**, 3–13 (1993).

52. A. Ciabrera, E. D. Zitti, and G. M. Bisio, Molecular information processing and physical constraints on computation, *Chemtronics*, **5**, 17–22 (1991).

53. M. Conrad, Biomolecular information processing, *IEEE Potentials*, 12–15 (1987).

54. M. Conrad, The seed germination model of enzyme catalysis, *BioSystems*, **27**, 223–233 (1992).

55. J. M. Valleton, Information processing in biomolecular-based biomimetic systems: from macroscopic to nanoscopic scale, *React. Polym.*, **12**, 109–131 (1990).

56. F. T. Hong, Do biomolecules process information differently than synthetic organic molecules? *BioSystems*, **27**, 189–194 (1992).

57. D. Bray, Protein molecules as computational elements in living cells, *Nature*, **376**, 307–312 (1995).

58. B. Crabtree, A metabolic switch produced by enzymatically interconvertible forms of an enzyme, *FEBS Lett.*, **187**(2), 193–195 (1985).

59. G. Ashkenazy, Biochemical molecular logic systems: structure and function, M.Sc. thesis, Technion (Israel Institute of Technology), Haifa, Israel, 1992.

60. I. Willner, S. Rubin, and T. Zor, Photoregulation of α-chymotrypsin by its immobilization in a photochromic azobenzene copolymer, *J. Am. Chem. Soc.*, **113**, 4013–4014 (1991).

61. I. Willner, S. Rubin, and A. Riklin, Photoregulation of papain activity through anchoring photochromic azo groups to the enzyme backbone, *J. Am. Chem. Soc.*, **113**, 3321–3325 (1991).

62. S. Tuchman, Biochemical systems for molecular logic elements, D.Sc. thesis, Technion (Israel Institute of Technology), Haifa, Israel, 1993.

63. S. Tuchman, S. Sideman, S. Kenig, and N. Lotan, Enzyme based logic gates controlled by outside signals: principles and design, in *Molecular Electronics and Molecular Electronic Devices*, K. Sienicki, Ed., Vol. III, CRC Press, Boca Raton, FL, 1994, pp. 223–238.

64. S. Sivan, Biochemical logic systems in molecular electronics: enzyme based systems, M.Sc. thesis, Technion (Israel Institute of Technology), Haifa, Israel, 1995.

65. A. Aoki, M. Ueda, H. Nakajima, and A. Tanaka, Construction of a photo controllable enzyme reaction system by co-immobilization of an enzyme and a semiconductor, *Biocatalysis*, **2**, 89–95 (1989).

66. T. Aoki, M. Kameyama, and T. Higuchi, Interconnection free biomolecular computing, *Computer*, **11**, 41–49 (1992).

67. M. Conrad, Molecular computing: the lock-key paradigm, *Computer*, **11**, 11–20 (1992).

68. D. Bray and S. Lay, Computer simulated evolution of a network of cell signaling molecules, *Biophys. J.*, **66**, 972–977 (1994).

69. F. T. Hong, The bacteriorhodopsin model membrane system as a prototype molecular computing element, *BioSystems*, **19**, 223–236 (1986).

70. G. I. Groma, G. Szabo, G. Varo, F. Raski, and L. Keszthelyi, Bacteriorhodopsin: a picosecond optoelectric signal transducer, *BioSystems*, **27**, 201–202 (1992).

71. H. Szu, A. Tate, D. Cullin, M. Walch, D. Demske, J. Garcia, S. Phuvan, and N. Caviris, Molecular computing for edge-enhanced laser imaging, *BioSystems*, **27**, 179–188 (1992).

72. N. Hampp and D. Zeisel, Mutated bacteriorhodopsin, *IEEE Eng. Med. Biol.*, **13**(1), 67–74 (1994).

73. F. T. Hong, Photovoltaic effects in biomembranes, *IEEE Eng. Med. Biol.*, **13**(1), 75–93 (1994).

74. D. K. Gifford, On the path to computation with DNA, *Science*, **266**, 993–994 (1994).

75. L. M. Adleman, Molecular computation of solutions to combinatorial problems, *Science*, **266**, 1021–1024 (1994).

76. M. Okamoto, A. Katsurayama, M. Tsukiji, Y. Aso, and K. Hayashi, Dynamic behaviour of enzymatic system realizing two-factor model, *J. Theor. Biol.*, **83**, 1–16 (1980).

77. M. Okamoto and K. Hayashi, Dynamic behaviour of cyclic enzyme systems, *J. Theor. Biol.*, **104**, 591–598 (1983).

78. M. Okamoto and K. Hayashi, Optimal control mode of a biochemical feedback system, *BioSystems.*, **16**, 315–321 (1984).

79. M. Okamoto and K. Hayashi, Control mechanism for a bacterial sugar-transport system: theoretical hypothesis, *J. Theor. Biol.*, **113**, 785–790 (1985).

80. M. Okamoto, T. Sakai, and K. Hayashi, Switching mechanism of a cyclic enzyme system: role as a "chemical diode," *BioSystems*, **21**, 1–11 (1987).

81. M. Okamoto, T. Sakai, and K. Hayashi, Biochemical switching device realizing McCulloch–Pitts type equation, *Biol. Cybern.*, **58**, 295–299 (1988).

82. M. Okamoto, T. Sakai, and K. Hayashi, Biochemical switching device: mono-cyclic enzyme system, *Biotechnol. Bioeng.*, **32**, 527–537 (1988).

83. M. Okamoto, T. Sakai, and K. Hayashi, Biochemical switching device: how to turn on (off) the switch, *BioSystems*, **22**, 155–162 (1989).

84. M. Okamoto and K. Hayashi, Network study of integrated biochemical systems: I. Connection of basic elements, *BioSystems*, **24**, 39–52 (1990).

85. M. Okamoto, Biochemical switching device: biomimetic approach and application to neural network study, *J. Biotechnol.*, **109**, 109–127 (1992).

86. M. Okamoto, Y. Maki, T. Sekiguchi, and S. Yoshida, Self-organization in a biochemical-neuron network, *Physica D: Nonlinear Phenomena*, **84**, 194–203 (1995).

87. O. H. Lowry, J. V. Passonneau, D. W. Schulz, and M. K. Rock, the measurement of pyridine nucleotides by enzymatic cycling, *J. Biol. Chem.*, **236**, 2746–2755 (1961).

88. S. Cha and C. J. M. Cha, Kinetics of cycling enzyme systems, *Mol. Pharmacol.*, **1**, 178–189 (1965).

89. L. E. Kopp and R. P. Miech, Nonlinear enzymatic cycling systems: the exponential cycling system, *J. Biol. Chem.*, **247**(11), 3558–3563 (1972).

90. F. Schubert, D. Kirstein, K. L. Schröder, and F. W. Scheller, Enzyme electrodes with substrate and coenzyme amplification, *Anal. Chim. Acta.*, **169**, 391–396 (1985).

91. I. Karube, K. Ikebukuro, Y. Murakami, and K. Yokoyama, Micromachining technology and biosensors, *Ann. N.Y. Acad. Sci.*, **750**, 101–108 (1995).

92. S. Uchiyama, H. Shimizu, and Y. Hasebe, Chemical amplification of uric acid sensor responses by dithiothreitol, *Anal. Chem.*, **66**, 1873–1876 (1994).

93. D. Pfeiffer, F. W. Scheller, C. J. McNeil, and T. Schulmeister, Cascade like exponential substrate amplification in enzyme sensors, *Biosensors Bioelectron.*, **10**, 169–180 (1995).

94. C. Burstein, H. Ounissi, M. D. Legoy, G. Gellf, and D. Thomas, Recycling of NAD using coimmobilized alcohol dehydrogenase and *E. coli*, *Appl. Biochem. Biotechnol.*, **6**, 329–338 (1981).

95. R. Wichmann and C. Wandrey, Continuous enzymatic transformation in an enzyme membrane reactor with simultaneous NAD(H) regeneration, *Biotechnol. Bioeng.*, **23**, 2789–2802 (1981).

96. E. Chave, E. Adamowicz, and C. Burstein, Recycling of NADP using immobilized *E. coli* and glucose-6-phosphate dehydrogenase, *Appl. Biochem. Biotechnol.*, **7**, 431–441 (1982).

97. O. Miyawaki, K. Nakamura, and T. Yano, Experimental investigation of continuous NAD recycling by conjugated enzymes immobilized in ultrafiltration hollow fiber, *J. Chem. Eng. Jpn.*, **15**(3), 224–228 (1982).

98. D. Mandler and I. Willner, Photosensitized NAD(P)H regeneration systems: application in the reduction of butan-2-one, pyruvic, and acetoacetic acids and in the reductive amination of pyruvic and oxoglutaric acids to amino acids, *J. Chem. Soc. Perkin Trans. II*, 805–811 (1986).

99. W. Berke, H. J. Schuz, C. Wandrey, M. Morr, G. Denda, and M. R. Kula, Continuous regeneration of ATP in enzyme membrane reactor for enzymatic synthesis, *Biotechnol. Bioeng.*, **32**, 130–139 (1988).

100. M. Howaldt, A. Gottlob, K. D. Kulbe, and H. Chmiel, Simultaneous conversion of glucose/fructose mixtures in a membrane reactor, *Ann. N.Y. Acad. Sci.*, **542**, 400–405 (1988).

101. H. Ishikawa, S. Takase, T. Tanaka, and H. Hikita, Experimental investigation of G6P production and simultaneous ATP regeneration by conjugated enzymes

in an ultrafiltration hollow fiber reactor, *Biotechnol. Bioeng.*, **34**, 369–379 (1989).

102. K. F. Gu and T. M. S. Chang, Conversion of ammonia or urea into L-leucine, L-valine and L-isoleucine using artificial cells containing an immobilized multienzyme system and dextran-NAD⁺, glucose dehydrogenase for co-factor recycling, *ASAIO*, **11**(1), 24–28 (1988).

103. K. F. Gu and T. M. S. Chang, Production of essential L-branched-chain amino acids in bioreactors containing artificial cells immobilized multienzyme systems and dextran-NAD⁺, *Biotechnol. Bioeng.*, **36**, 263–269 (1990).

104. K. F. Gu and T. M. S. Chang, Conversion of ammonia or urea into essential amino acids, using artificial cells containing an immobilized multienzyme system and dextran-NAD⁺: 2. Yeast alcohol dehydrogenase for coenzyme recycling, *Biotechnol. Appl. Biochem.*, **12**, 227–236 (1990).

105. K. F. Gu and T. M. S. Chang, Conversion of ammonia or urea into essential amino acids, using artificial cells containing an immobilized multienzyme system and dextran-NAD⁺: IV. Malate dehydrogenase for coenzyme recycling, *J. Mol. Catal.*, **62**, 331–339 (1990).

106. O. Miyawaki and T. Yano, Dynamic affinity between dissociable coenzyme and immobilized enzyme in an affinity chromatographic reactor with single enzyme, *Biotechnol. Bioeng.*, **39**, 314–319 (1992).

107. G. X. Li and Y. M. He, Regeneration of NAD by conjugated mannitol dehydrogenase and glucose dehydrogenase systems, *Ann. N.Y. Acad. Sci.*, **750**, 15 (1995).

108. L. Wang and J. Ross, Synchronous neural networks of nonlinear threshold elements with hysteresis, *Proc. Natl. Acad. Sci. USA*, **87**, 988–992 (1990).

109. A. Hjelmfelt, E. D. Weinberger, and J. Ross, Chemical implementation of neural networks and Turing machines, *Proc. Natl. Acad. Sci. USA*, **88**, 10983–10987 (1991).

110. A. Hjelmfelt, E. D. Weinberger, and J. Ross, Chemical implementation of finite-state machines, *Proc. Natl. Acad. Sci. USA*, **89**, 383–387 (1992).

111. A. Hjelmfelt and J. Ross, Chemical implementation and thermodynamics of collective neural networks, *Proc. Natl. Acad. Sci. USA*, **89**, 388–391 (1992).

112. A. Hjelmfelt, F. W. Schneider, and J. Ross, Pattern recognition in coupled chemical kinetic systems, *Science*, **260**, 335–336 (1993).

113. A. Hjelmfelt and J. Ross, Mass coupled chemical systems with computational properties, *J. Phys. Chem.*, **97**, 7988–7992 (1993).

114. A. Hjelmfelt and J. Ross, Pattern recognition, chaos, and multiplicity in neural networks of excitable systems, *Proc. Natl. Acad. Sci. USA*, **91**, 63–37 (1994).

115. A. Arkin and J. Ross, Computational functions in biochemical reaction networks, *Biophys. J.*, **67**, 560–578 (1994).

116. A. Hjelmfelt and J. Ross, Implementation of logic functions and computations by chemical kinetics, *Physica D: Nonlinear Phenomena*, **84**, 180–193 (1995).

117. O. E. Rösler, A multivibrating switching network in homogeneous kinetics, *Bull. Math. Biol.*, **37**, 181–191 (1975).

118. P. Schnittker, On chemical oscillators responding a frequency switch, *J. Non-Equilib. Thermodyn.*, **5**, 129–136 (1980).

119. A. Goldbeter and D. E. Koshland, Jr., An amplified sensitivity arising from covalent modification in biological systems, *Proc. Natl. Acad. Sci. USA*, **78**(11), 6840–6844 (1981).

120. D. C. LaPorte and D. E. Koshland, Jr., Phosphorylation of isocitrate dehydrogenase as a demonstration of enhaced sensitivity in covalent regulation, *Nature*, **305**, 286–290 (1983).

121. J. E. Lisman, A mechanism for memory storage insensitive to molecular turnover: a bistable autophosphorylating kinase, *Proc. Natl. Acad. Sci. USA*, **82**, 3055–3057 (1985).

122. D. E. Koshland, Jr., Switches, thresholds and ultrasensitivity, *TIBS*, **12**, 225–229 (1987).

123. B. Hess and A. Boiteux, Oscillations in biochemical systems, *Ber. Bunsen-Ges. Phys. Chem.*, **84**, 346–351 (1980).

124. P. E. Rapp, Frequency encoded biochemical regulation is more accurate than amplitude dependent control, *J. Theor. Biol.*, **90**, 531–544 (1981).

125. A. Goldbeter, G. Dupont, and M. Berridge, Minimal model for signal induced Ca^{2+} oscillations and for their frequency encoding through protein phosphorylation, *Proc. Natl. Acad. Sci. USA*, **87**, 1461–1465 (1990).

126. A. Goldbeter, Pulsatile signaling as an optimal mode of intercellular communication, *Proc. Int. Symp. Control. Release Bioact. Mater.*, **22**, 107–108 (1995).

127. J. P. Baker and R. A. Siegel, Poly(*N*-isopropylacrylamide) hydrogel membranes for pulsatile drug delivery, *Proc. Int. Symp. Control. Release Bioact. Mater.*, **22**, 340–341 (1995).

128. R. A. Siegel, Membrane based oscillatory drug delivery: models, *Proc. Int. Symp. Control. Release Bioact. Mater.*, **22**, 109–110 (1995).

129. R. A. Siegel, X. Zou, and J. P. Baker, Periodic pulsatile delivery based on membrane hysteresis: theory, *Proc. Int. Symp. Control. Release Bioact. Mater.*, **22**, 115–116 (1995).

130. J. P. Baker and R. A. Siegel, Hysteresis in the glucose permeability versus pH characteristic for a responsive hydrogel membrane, *Macromol. Rapid Commun.*, **17**, 409–415 (1996).

131. R. A. Siegel, Modeling of self-regulating oscillatory drug delivery, in *Controlled Release: Challenges and Strategies*, K. Park, Ed., American Chemical Society, Washington, DC, 1997.

132. L. Glaser and D. H. Brown, Purification and properties of D-glucose-6-phosphate dehydrogenase, *J. Biol. Chem.*, **216**, 67–79 (1955).

133. H. J. Engel, W. Domschke, M. Alberti, and G. F. Domagk, Protein structure and enzymatic activity: II. Purification and properties of a crystalline glucose-6-phosphate dehydrogenase from *Candida utilis*, *Biochim. Biophys. Acta*, **191**, 509–522 (1969).

134. R. D. Mavis and E. Stellwagen, Purification and subunit structure of glutathione reductase from bakers' yeast, *J. Biol. Chem.*, **243**(4), 809–814 (1968).

135. I. Ii and H. Sakai, Glutathione reductase in the sea urchin egg: I. Purification and general properties, *Biochim. Biophys. Acta*, **350**, 141–150 (1974).

136. N. G. Brink, Beef liver glucose dehydrogenase: I. Purification and properties, *Acta Chem. Scand.*, **7**(7), 1081–1097 (1953).

137. H. J. Strecker and S. Korkes, Glucose dehydrogenase, *J. Biol. Chem.*, **196**, 769–784 (1952).

138. R. P. Metzger, S. S. Wilcox, and A. N. Wick, Studies with rat liver glucose dehydrogenase, *J. Biol. Chem.*, **239**(6), 1769–1772 (1964).

139. H. E. Pauly and G. Pfleiderer, D-Glucose dehydrogenase from *Bacillus megaterium* M 1286: purification, properties and structure, *Hoppe–Seyler's Z. Physiol. Chem.*, **356**, 1613–1623 (1975).

140. M. Romano and M. Cerra, The action of crystalline lactate dehydrogenase from rabbit muscle on glyoxylate, *Biochim. Biophys. Acta*, **177**, 421–426 (1969).

141. M. T. Hakala, A. J. Glaid, and G. W. Schwert, Lactic dehydrogenase, *J. Biol. Chem.*, **221**, 191–209 (1956).

142. V. Zewe and H. J. Fromm, Kinetic studies of rabbit muscle lactate dehydrogenase, *J. Biol. Chem.*, **237**(5), 1668–1675 (1962).

143. D. Dennis and N. O. Kaplan, D- and L-Lactic acid dehydrogenases in *Lactobacillus plantarum*, *J. Biol. Chem.*, **235**(3), 810–818 (1960).

144. C. J. Dickenson and F. M. Dickinson, A study of pH and temperature dependence of the reaction of yeast alcohol dehydrogenase with ethanol, acetaldehyde and butyraldehyde, *Biochem. J.*, **147**, 303–311 (1975).

145. L. Brand, *Differential and Difference Equations*, Wiley, New York, 1966, pp. 359–363.

146. I. H. Segel, *Enzyme Kinetics, Behavior and Analysis of Rapid Equilibrium and Steady-State Enzyme Systems*, Wiley, New York, 1975.

147. A. R. Schulz, *Enzyme Kinetics, From Diastase to Multi Enzyme Systems*, Cambridge University Press, New York, 1994.

148. S. Guzy, Enzymic reactors for biomedical uses: engineering aspects, D.Sc. thesis, Technion (Israel Institute of Technology), Haifa, Israel, 1989.

149. E. M. Scott, I. W. Duncan, and V. Ekstrand, Purification and properties of glutathione reductase of human erythrocytes, *J. Biol. Chem.*, **238**(12), 3928–3933 (1963).

150. M. L. Minsky, *Computation: Finite and Infinite Machines*, Prentice-Hall, Engelwood Cliffs, NJ, 1967.

151. J. E. Hopcroft and J. D. Ullman, *Introduction to Automata Theory, Languages, and Computation*, Addison-Wesley, Reading, MA 1979.

152. H. T. Siegelmann and E. D. Sontag, On the computational power of neural nets, *J. Comput. Syst. Sci.*, **50**(1), 132–150 (1995).

153. H. T. Siegelmann, Computation beyond the Turing limit, *Science*, **268**, 545–548 (1995).

154. H. T. Siegelmann, Computability with neural networks, *Lect. Appl. Math.*, **32**, 733–747 (1996).

155. J. L. Balcazar, R. Gavalda, and H. T. Siegelmann, Computational power of neural networks: a Kolmogorov complexity characterization, *IEEE Trans. Inf. Theory* (1997).

156. J. Kilian and H. T. Siegelmann, The dynamic universality of sigmoidal neural networks, *Inf. Comput.*, **128**(1), 48–56 (1996).

157. M. B. Pour-El, Abstract computability and its relation to the general purpose analog computer, *Bull. Am. Math. Soc.*, **199**, 1–28 (1974).

158. L. A. Rubel, A universal differential equation, *Bull. Am. Math. Soc.*, **4**(3), 345–349 (1981).

159. L. A. Rubel, The extended analog computer, *Adv. Appl. Math.*, **14**, 39–50 (1993).

INDEX

Information Processing by Biochemical Systems: Neural Network–Type Configurations, By Orna Filo and Noah Lotan
Copyright © 2010 John Wiley & Sons, Inc.